Starting Your
Career as a
Theatrical Designer

Michael J. Riha

Starting Your Career as a Theatrical Designer

Insights and Advice from Leading Broadway Designers

by Michael J. Riha

Foreword by Michael Mayer

ALLWORTH PRESS
NEW YORK

Allworth Press books may be purchased in bulk at special discounts for sales promotion, corporate gifts, fund-raising, or educational purposes. Special editions can also be created to specifications. For details, contact the Special Sales Department, Allworth Press, 307 West 36th Street, 11th Floor, New York, NY 10018 or info@skyhorsepublishing.com.

15 14 13 12 11   5 4 3 2 1

Published by Allworth Press, an imprint of Skyhorse Publishing, Inc.

307 West 36th Street, 11th Floor, New York, NY 10018.

Allworth Press® is a registered trademark of Skyhorse Publishing, Inc.®, a Delaware corporation.

www.allworth.com

Cover design by Mary Belibasakis
Cover photo courtesy of Doug Hamilton

Library of Congress Cataloging-in-Publication Data is available on file.
ISBN: 978-1-58115-908-0

Printed in China

To my Mom and Dad. You are,
and have always been, my rock.

CONTENTS

FOREWORD

When Michael Riha invited me to write the foreword to this invaluable collection of interviews, I agreed without a moment's hesitation, even though, at that time, I hadn't read a single one of them. The fact is, I love designers and have always wondered, "How do they do that voodoo that they do so well?" When I received the manuscript, I thought I'd give it a quick look before bed and then really go through it when I had more time—however, it didn't work out that way. I tore through it, ravenously, and in one sitting. I was mesmerized and genuinely humbled. We directors look to our designers to make manifest the often inchoate dreams we grasp at remembering in the daylight, the elusive chasing of images, feelings, energies, metaphors, and stories that coexist alongside and inside the dramatic texts we grapple to understand. The relationship between a director and his or her designers is essential, provocative, and intimate. It practically defines the word "collaboration"; and yet, how often do we ask ourselves about the solitary nature of the designer's efforts? How do they create the environment where they do their work?

Many of these remarkable designers are my own most frequent and beloved collaborators. Indeed, several of them are my earliest partners in the adventure of carving out a career in the theatre, and have influenced my life and art in profound ways. Some of them are not only artists with whom I am working steadily as I write this, but also among my very best friends. All of them are designers whose work I know very well and respect; yet, as I read the interviews in this book, I feel like I am meeting them and their work for the very first time. Their own relationship to their art, and in particular the way they make their lives work so that their best creative impulses can flourish, is a continual revelation.

Their designs speak for themselves; however, these interviews tell wonderfully personal stories with clarity, honesty, humor, and passion. I invite you to read and admire the unique journeys that brought them to the theatre, marvel at their tenacity and bravery as they re-invent themselves, and learn from their mistakes and triumphs. Look to these fine artists for varied ways to maintain not only careers, but fulfilling lives in the theatre as well. They are intrepid explorers of new theatrical landscapes and interpreters and translators of stories that demand dramatic articulation. They are also the inventors of new ideas that illuminate our stages and our understanding of ourselves and the world we live in—a world we see changing all the time and a world we all hope to change for the better with the theatre we create.

  This book is not only a fabulous user's manual for young designers who are just beginning their own careers and theatre lovers who want to know how it all works, but also for all of us who seek inspiration wherever we can find it. This is the mother lode.

—Michael Mayer

ACKNOWLEDGMENTS

I need to begin by thanking Michael Mayer and all of the designers who are featured in this book. Without your generosity, candor, and incredibly inspiring words, this book would not have been possible. I am humbled by and grateful for the new friendships I have made; I will forever be indebted to each and every one of you. I would also be remiss if I didn't thank all of the photographers who contributed such beautiful images. Your work is much appreciated.

I would also like to thank Tad Crawford, my publisher, for deciding to make that phone call and take a chance on a book that I know will help to change the lives of generations of young, hopeful designers. I also want to thank my editor, Delia Casa, for her patience and willingness to guide me through this daunting process.

In addition, I owe a debt of gratitude to my current and former students. For the past twenty years, you have served as my greatest inspiration. It is because of you that I believed it was necessary to write a book that would encourage you to follow your dreams, no matter how out of reach they may seem. If this kid from Antigo, Wisconsin can achieve so many of his dreams—even finding his way into a Broadway theatre and working with some of the most inspiring, talented, and kind people in the business (thank you Christine, Michael, and Kevin)—then anyone can. This is for all of you who have come through the University of Arkansas' department of drama and for those I've yet to have the honor to instruct.

And finally, I want to thank you, Anne, for serving as my writing coach, transcribing partner, and head cheerleader when I thought I would never find a publisher. To you, I am forever indebted.

INTRODUCTION

I have wanted to write a book featuring successful theatre designers
for quite a while, but my major concern was the selection process.
Who would be in, and who would be left out? Although this process
was incredibly difficult, the designers I eventually elected to include
come from all walks of life and boast successful careers in both commercial theatre and the not-for-profit sector. Of the close to seventy
shows that were on Broadway during the 2010–2011 season, nearly
40 percent of all shows featured at least one of the ten designers
profiled in this book. Moreover, if the difficulty I had fixing a time to
meet with them is any indication of their reputation and workload, it
appears they are well on their way to securing very long and successful careers. In addition to their more visible work on the Great White
Way, all of these designers have successful careers off-Broadway, at
regional theatres across the country and, in some cases, internationally
as well. I found each and every one of them to be incredibly generous
with their time as well as surprisingly encouraging about the opportunities available to young designers when it comes to working in
perhaps the most recognized and scrutinized theatre community in the
world—New York City.

     Given the extraordinarily high expectations of today's so-
phisticated theatre audiences and the gradual increase in technology
as part of the live theatre experience, all of the designers were in
complete agreement on one thing: The world of theatre design has
changed dramatically over the past twenty years. With ticket prices
ranging anywhere from $30 to $600 for VIP seating, never before
has there been so much pressure to deliver a product that showcases
outstanding performances as well as show-stopping production values.
Gone are the days of cumbersome, oversized scenic wagons pushed
across the stage by technicians. Today, computer-controlled scenic
units with pneumatic and hydraulic technology glide across the stage
with virtual ease. Scenic backdrops that were once hand painted are
being replaced with digital printouts, projections, and LED screens.
Automated lighting fixtures have also replaced many of the traditional
lighting fixtures. All Broadway designers must be familiar with these
new methods in order to successfully maneuver the complicated and

highly sophisticated world of design for the Broadway stage. Through all of these technological advances, however, one fixation that has remained constant is the commitment to create the most beautiful stage pictures imaginable. These ten designers' primary goal is just that—to provide stunningly evocative environments for presenting each and every story to the audience.

The interviews lasted two to three hours and were conducted either in the designer's studio or his or her apartment, with the occasional meeting at a New York City restaurant. What you will be reading is the distillation of the thoughts, ideas, and memories of unique paths through the world of commercial and not-for-profit theatre, as told by a group of incredibly talented, articulate, and passionate people, whose contribution to the audiences' experience is essential.

My primary intention in writing this book was to illustrate, through the stories of ten exceptionally successful individuals, that there are many "paths" one can take to achieve fulfillment in this extremely competitive business. Even though there are similarities between each of the designers, it is clear that there is no "right answer" when it comes to the question, "How can I make it as a theatre designer?" When I began interviewing, it quickly became clear that the best way to have a rich dialogue was to allow each designer to "guide" me through his or her path rather than direct the conversation with a series of stock questions. The interviews are filled with professional advice, design experience, academic opportunities, and, often overlooked but absolutely necessary, tips on how to stay healthy in this high-stress industry. I hope you find their unique stories as inspiring and informative as I do.

—*Michael J. Riha, Fayetteville, AR*

Part I: Set Designers

DAVID GALLO – SET DESIGNER
Monday, March 14, 2011

David Gallo began his career working in the film industry as a painter in the art department, but he quickly found that his true "home" was in the theatre. As a "military kid," David lived abroad until the age of ten, when he moved to Long Island. He remained in the New York metropolitan area during his school years and has been a NYC resident since 1987. David has worked with a number of notable regional theatres, including the Cincinnati Playhouse in the Park, Goodspeed Opera House, La Jolla Playhouse, and the Pittsburgh Public Theatre.

In addition to his work on the Broadway stage he has a wonderfully successful career overseas, where he has designed productions across Europe in cities such as Amsterdam, Antwerp, Hamburg, Berlin, Milan, and Rome to name just a few. An especially noteworthy distinction is David's long-term relationship with the late August Wilson. He designed all of the premieres of August Wilson's later works and was also selected to design the tribute production, "August Wilson's Twentieth Century" at the Kennedy Center in Washington DC in 2008.

Q: Did you grow up with theatre as part of your life?

A: We didn't go to the theatre a great deal and I certainly didn't come from one of those cosmopolitan families like Jo Meilzener's family, where his mother was the editor of *Vogue Paris*, and his family would summer in the south of France. Our family was nothing like that. From the point when my dad moved on and my mother raised us, we struggled financially.

I was brought to the theatre several times as a child, just like any other event you might take a young boy to when he is growing up; I actually remember those experiences quite vividly. When I started to become more interested in theatre, my mother became very conscious of trying to provide me with the necessary experiences that would be fundamental to my cultural growth. Tickets were always expensive—too expensive—but my mother cared enough to make it work. I remember one specific moment when *Cats* opened. Gosh, that must have been when I was a sophomore in high school. Looking back on it now, seeing *Cats* was such a remarkable experience for me. Also, Cameron Mackintosh brilliantly promoted it in such a way that everyone believed if you didn't see *Cats* you lacked any sort of legitimacy as a human being. At that time, a Broadway ticket was very expensive and we were pretty broke, yet my mother piled up enough money so I could go and see it. I remember sitting in the worst seat in the house, but it didn't matter. It wasn't like I said to her, "I must see *Cats*!" She just thought, and probably rightfully so, that it was necessary for me to see it to help round out my interests. Occasionally, I would see other shows in New York.

Q: When did you first get interested in theatre?

A: I did theatre when I was in high school. I was also really into film at that time, too. I didn't know what I wanted to do, but I was really interested in movies. I thought the design aspects of film were always very interesting, especially the process of filmmaking. I was strongly influenced by the movies I saw and the environments within the films. I remember, even back then, being fascinated by the concept of scenery. I loved that the worlds created for these movies were fake; it was just wood and canvas and cardboard.

Then, in 1977, when I was eleven years old, *Star Wars* came out and that was very influential. This movie was being targeted toward my exact age group and George Lucas also did something that was quite unique. He took the archives from the art department for *Star Wars,* as well as his other films, and published the art director's drawings in large-scale art books. This was incredibly interesting to me. Here was this guy who created this completely believable fantasy world and he was giving away the secret. He was showing where these characters came from and where they lived. He also shared the sketches of these amazing sets and explained where all of his ideas came from. I would spend all of my time recreating those drawings from the age of eleven up to, gosh, certainly way too old to be doing it! I probably should have had other interests, but I just loved re-drafting and re-sketching those drawings. That's really what led me to have an interest in designing. Seeing *Star Wars* and learning to draw from that book changed everything. I began to realize that it was someone's job to come up with the designs for movies.

On my very first day of high school, I went into an art class and met a man who would be my mentor throughout my entire time in high school. I remember one day he said to me, "Why don't you come to the theatre on Saturday and help us out?" They happened to be doing a production of *Pippin* and I said, "OK." It was an incredible experience. Here we were: making scenery, building and painting stuff, and it was right there on the stage. From that moment on, I decided that theatre was for me. I never looked back.

Q: Why theatre instead of filmmaking?

A: For one thing, making a movie was virtually inaccessible for a young person back then. Sure, I made my Super 8 movies like everybody else, but it was such a pain in the ass. Today, anybody with a two-hundred-dollar computer and a phone that shoots video is "Steven Spielberg." Back then, when I was eleven years old, you couldn't really make a movie. I did make animated shorts and stuff like that, but here, in the theatre, I was telling complete stories.

Q: Once you changed your focus from film to theatre, what additional opportunities did you pursue to develop your skills?

A: Once theatre became my passion, I began seeing as much of it as possible. I also read as many books about theatre as I could get my hands on, and I really started studying design. I went from replicating the *Star Wars* drawings to replicating theatre design drawings. For a while, I was an intern at a summer theatre and I would steal the drafting out of the dumpster after we had built the set. I would take the drawings back to my room where I had a drafting table set up, unfold these old sheets of drafting, and replicate them. I also had a library card and remember checking out a textbook on drafting. The text was from the 1940s or something, but I didn't know any different; that's all they had at the library. I also remember that it wasn't even a theatre-drafting book. It was called "Technical Drawing for the Young Man" or something like that. I remember that it had instructions on how to sharpen your pencils with a razor blade and how to keep your hair tonic from dripping on your drawings! Seriously, it had drawings of some guy leaning over his drafting, and his hair tonic was dripping all over his work, ruining it. Replicating drawings and copying other designers' drafting was what eventually led me to draw and design my own scenery.

When it came time for me to apply to college, I knew what I wanted to do and I found SUNY Purchase. It was also necessary for me financially, as well as academically, to go to a State University of New York. The way the state schools are set up in New York is there are a number of schools, each with different specialties, and SUNY Purchase was the one for theatre.

Q: Did you go on to graduate school after you got your degree from SUNY?

A: I didn't go to graduate school. As a matter of fact, I didn't even finish college. My academic experience was somewhat complicated. I certainly learned a lot of wonderful things while I was in college, but at that time in my life I didn't have the tools needed in order to exist in an academic environment. I would love to be able to say the reason I didn't quite fit into the restrictions of the conservative confines of academia was because I was so interesting, and that I had too many radical ideas as a designer. Sadly, none of that was true. I just didn't have the ability to fit into a traditional training program. I feel like it was actually the structure that was hampering me from progressing as a designer. It wasn't until after I got out of school and started working in the field using my own tools and methods that the design process worked for me.

Q: Was it a difficult transition going right from undergraduate school to New York since you didn't go to graduate school, where so many of those professional relationships are cultivated?

A: That's true. I didn't really have any of that relationship building because, I believe, so much of that really does have to do with the graduate school model. Graduate school seems to be where you go to meet other student directors and student playwrights and you create a peer group, and you all move forward together from there. That wasn't available at SUNY, mainly because they didn't have either a directing or a playwriting program. What they did have was a very intense conservatory training program for design and production—it was an amazing school for that kind of training. You really learned about the technical process, but it wasn't set up to offer undergraduate students the same kind of experience you'd get when you go to graduate school. I did, however, learn how to build models and draft scenery really well, along with all of the other practical aspects of technical theatre.

Q: Did you intend on getting a degree?

A: I fully expected to graduate, but it just didn't happen. Basically, enough was enough, and I was done. I walked away from college right before I would have graduated. My mother works as a social worker in academia where credentials are very important. My mother was upset and always believed that my lack of a degree was going to be very damaging to my future plans. She didn't find out until later that it was not that big of an issue.

Q: Did you have another job outside of the theatre that you used to pay your bills? Or have you always worked in the theatre?

A: Oddly enough, my earliest jobs were working on movies. That's the work that paid my bills. While I was a student at SUNY Purchase, I spent so much time in the scenery shops, prop shops, and paint shops, as well as drafting scenery, that I developed really great skills in those areas and was highly employable. When I got out of school, through my reputation and my connections, I was able to get all sorts of jobs. My pager would go off, and I'd get a job art-directing a television commercial.

One day I got a call from a production designer working on a Brooke Shields movie to paint graffiti all over Jersey City and Hoboken. I had been doing graffiti and scenic design since I was young, and in less than twenty-four hours after that phone call, I was on a one-hundred-foot extension ladder with two hundred cans of spray paint! I also remember that job paid about $1,000 a day, which was better than I had ever been paid in my life.

Back then, I would do anything that kept me in the industry. For the most part, my early design experiences afforded me a simple existence whereby I lived hand to mouth, and I survived by taking one silly job after another. It really was a life of jumping back and forth between working on films, working on television, and all sorts of different projects. I was also very fortunate to be able to focus on my own career as a designer as well. I soon began to realize that I was doing all of this work for other designers; I was always "the worker," but I wanted to be the designer.

Q: Were there designers that you looked up to and wanted to work for when you came to New York after SUNY?

A: I did, and I turned out to be wrong. I pulled out the *American Set Design* book and wrote to three different designers whose philosophies matched mine, or so I thought. Out of the three designers, one never called me back; another called me back to say he didn't use assistants. I had just designed a show at a regional theatre where he had been hired to design right after me, and the set I had designed was grossly over scaled and he called just to tell me that. . . . He said, "I just want you to know that, that set was the biggest thing I had ever seen in my entire life." It was sort of a good-natured ribbing from one designer to another.

I actually went to meet with the third designer I had written to, and he tended to be hung up on some of the unique ways I approached design. Basically, he was appalled by my lack of an academic background. The interview was somewhat strange; however, when he saw my portfolio and that I was actually a working designer, he was more encouraging when I said, "I'm not here to show you my design work; I'm here to show you my assistant skills." I had just gotten into the Union so my drafting was very tight. Eventually when he saw the slides of some of the productions I had done at some major regional theatres, he quickly became more encouraging. So, to finally answer your question, yes, I did look to other, more established designers with whom I might be able to find some work, but nothing ever really came of it.

Q: You were a young man when you first started. Did you find your young age put you at a disadvantage in this industry?

Actually, one of my advantages was that I always looked about ten or fifteen years older than I was. I'll say this right now—that didn't hurt. When I was in meetings, people saw in me someone who was thirty-five, even though I was only twenty-three. I had a monster, Grizzly Adams beard and huge hair and I looked much older than I was.

I remember sitting at a conference table where I was the associate on a musical that was going to be one of the biggest shows to ever be produced on Broadway and the project had gotten off to a pretty late start. The producers wanted the show to open by Tony nominations, so they all turned to me as the person in charge and literally let me decide whether this particular show was going to be able to open in time. Later during the meeting, I mentioned how I had seen *Cats* in the ninth grade and someone asked me, "Just how old are you?" So I told them, and everybody in the room was like, "Oh my God! We just let this idiot twenty-three-year-old kid make this decision!" Everyone in the room thought I was in my thirties, not some twenty-three-year-old. Now that's not to say I was all that mature or that I was a grown-up, I just had an advantage because I looked older.

Q: So how did you break into the commercial world of theatre?

A: In addition to all of the freelance work, I did some assisting for Jim Youmans, who was a senior in college when I was a freshman at SUNY. His career was just getting rolling and I wanted to help him out. Jim was close to my age, but five years more established. Working with him on various projects was exciting, and during that period of time, Jim was also assisting John Arnone. It was through Jim that I had an opportunity to briefly work for John Arnone. Through Jim, I had the opportunity to draft and build models for John. This opened the door for me to become John's assistant for *Tommy*, which was pivotal in my career.

Up to this point, I had a pretty good career designing productions regionally and the occasional off-off-Broadway or off-Broadway project. I also established a really great roster of directors with whom

I was working, including Christopher Ashley, Michael Greif, and Michael Mayer; we were all slowly moving up the "New York theatre ladder" quite nicely. Even though I was completely small potatoes, my career was starting to look pretty good. *Tommy* opened my eyes to commercial theatre and how Broadway works, which is completely different from anything you can possibly imagine. In fact, Broadway is different than any theatre on Planet Earth. I also took *Tommy* all over the world as the associate designer.

My previous goal, which was to live off of designing about twelve regional shows a year, suddenly took a 180-degree turn toward commercial theatre. Now, I wanted a life, a career, working on Broadway. It was that wonderful experience of working on *Tommy* that introduced me to the commercial theatre world. I was meeting general managers and producers and theatre owners, and all of these different types of people whom I had never met before. A whole new world was opening up to me, and it was all happening at the age of twenty-five. I began to see just how different commercial theatre was from not-for-profit theatre, and it gave me the necessary information and tools I needed to exist in that world.

Q: Do you remember your first commercial design?

While this was going on, a dear friend of mine was hired to direct the national tour of *Angels in America*, and he wanted me to design it. Typically with big-time producers, they will hire big-time designers. So when a young director says to them, "I want to hire this young designer friend of mine," the producers would normally just say, "Um, no. You need to use one of our established people because you are the new guy and we don't know him and there's a lot of money at stake." Instead, they said, "Oh, we know David. Sure." And that's how I ended up designing a major first national tour at a young age.

"*Tommy* opened my eyes to commercial theatre and how Broadway works, which is completely different from anything you can possibly imagine."

Q: Aside from the National Tour design job, when or how did your first Broadway gig come about?

A: I was designing shows that began generating more and more attention to my own work, which meant more and more directors wanted to work with me. So as *Tommy* was being phased out, as all shows are, my own stuff started taking off. Luckily, it was a completely seamless transition. The same producers who did *Tommy* also did *Titanic,* and they asked me to get involved with that show as well. At that point, I was really sort of done with assisting, but I took the job anyway. *Titanic* had a British associate designer, but they don't really do the same sort of work we do here in the United States. *Titanic* was incredibly complicated so they hired me to figure out how the set would *actually* go into our theatre. I signed on as the American associate (for lack of a better title), and I was able to take these brilliant design concepts and make them a concrete reality so they would work within the confines of a Broadway stage.

As I was phasing out my associate work for *Titanic,* I was also designing the off-Broadway play *Bunny Bunny,* which opened to some rather wonderful reviews. *Bunny Bunny* was kind of my breakout show back in 1997. I had already worked on Broadway, but *Bunny Bunny* really was the show that garnered a great deal of recognition, and new directors took notice.

Q: There are many differences between designing for not-for-profit theatre and commercial theatre such as Broadway. Can you talk about those differences?

A: Well, it's funny because even though I said that and believe it to be true, what immediately pops into my head are all of the ways they are similar. Regional theatres have a very particular approach, whether it's the tiniest theatre or the largest theatre in the country. They have their own production staffs that in some cases have been working together for a very long time. They also have specific slots: Main stage I, Main stage II, that sort of thing, and ultimately you are brought in as either the new person on the team or maybe you've been working there for years so you're looked at as an old family member. Whatever the case happens to be, you're fitting yourself into an entire season. So in a way, you have to follow their rules.

You're usually going into a finite space with finite money and finite time; everything is locked in. You're going to come in and fit into a certain mold; nevertheless, artistic concerns are the very highest. I won't say that not-for-profit theatres don't depend on ticket sales to make money, but ticket sales are only one financial component and it usually isn't the largest one.

Broadway, on the other hand, is a for-profit business; however, it's not nearly as cutthroat and mercenary as some people make it out to be. There are not many people producing on Broadway just to make a buck because it's quite possibly the most ill advised way to make a living. Of course, shows want to be successful and turn a profit, but the notion that all of these shows are produced by some big guy sitting in an office in Times Square, smoking a cigar, who only cares about the bottom line is not the norm. In fact, many producers are as creative as the talent they hire. You certainly have a different financial framework within which you work on Broadway as opposed to regional theatre, and although Broadway is completely commercially oriented, they still have the highest standards for the artistry as well. It's just a different producing model than regional theatre.

The way money is handled and allocated is also completely different on Broadway. For Broadway productions, budgets are typically determined long before the shows are designed, which can be problematic. You have a general manager, who puts together a budget, and then they hire a director and designers. Then, to complicate matters, the show turns out to be something completely different than what they had anticipated. It's strange because everyone involved with the production is trying to figure out what it's going to be, but everyone involved has his or her own agenda. Also, there really is no formula on Broadway; every show is its own entity—whereas in regional theatre they're able to say, "Well, here, we do it like this."

The biggest difference I find on Broadway is that there really is not the same system of checks and balances that exists in regional theatre. When you design for regional theatre, whether it is sets, lights, or sound, there are people who generally work in those theatres whose job it is to make sure what you have designed can actually happen. It's their job to make sure it fits into the space and that the necessary equipment is available. On Broadway, if your design doesn't fit, it's your fault. There are fantastic technical supervisors on Broadway, but the role of the regional technical director doesn't exist here. There's not really the same kind of safety net.

For Broadway productions, a sheet of drafting is a legal contract. The scenery shop—or many scenery shops, if the show is divided among several shops—has been contracted to build exactly what you have drawn without alteration. It does not have the same give-and-take as what happens at a regional theatre, where work is done under one roof. The scenic shops that build the Broadway shows will build whatever you draw without too many questions about the overall design. For example, if you draw a piece of scenery that won't fit into a regional theatre space, the resident technical director will usually say, "Hey, Dave, this won't fit into our theatre. Can you . . ." If you do that for a Broadway show, the scenic shops will build it as drawn, and when it arrives outside the door of the Richard Rodgers Theatre on 46th Street, they'll all be standing there saying, "Dave, it doesn't fit, now what?" And you, the designer, are responsible for all of those aspects, the fit as well as the function.

Also, on Broadway, you're always under a microscope. If you're doing a show at Seattle Rep it's a different ball game; everyone is in it to make it a success, and we want everyone to do his or her very best. It may sound paranoid, but on Broadway there are those who are looking to everyone else to fail—just a little bit. The whole community here is just not as universally supportive as it is in the regional theatre community. Also, on Broadway, you tend to be doing work that is new and has never been produced anywhere else, so the stakes to get it right the first time are very high.

There are also more players here on Broadway that you don't have regionally. For example, the general manager isn't a role you find at a regional theatre, but on Broadway the set designer and the general manager will become best friends (or worst enemies!) because you are going to spend so much time together. He's the main person responsible for keeping you financially in check, and it's your job to make sure the show is realized at the highest artistic level possible.

On Broadway, the designer tends to work directly with the commercial scenery shops, whose primary goal is to make money. They certainly are interested in pleasing the designer, but ultimately they are most interested in turning the greatest profit themselves; whereas in regional theatre shops, they are in the business to save money! They're there to figure out how to build something as inexpensively as possible. Commercial shops don't necessarily have to worry about that.

It takes some getting used to, but Broadway basically forms a new company for every show and in many ways reinvents the wheel for each production. On Broadway, you're always starting from scratch. What are we doing? Where are we doing it? Just this morning, before our interview, I was theatre shopping. I was literally going from theatre to theatre to theatre to pick where we should do a new, upcoming show. You certainly can't do that in a regional theatre!

Q: Are you saying that the set designer has a say in where the show will be opening on Broadway?

A: It depends. But, ordinarily, yes—especially if you have a hot show. Basically, the way that it works is if you're coming in with an awesome

Top: Production photo, David Gallo Design, Ltd.
Memphis, Shubert Theatre, New York, NY, 2009
Directed by Christopher Ashley
Lighting, Howell Binkley
Set, David Gallo
Bottom: Digital rendering, Steven C. Kemp

show or an incredible cast, the theatre owners will line up and say, "Pick me! Pick me!" So, you have currency. Sometimes that currency is a hot new show; sometimes it is two incredible star actors. Therefore, I can go into the theatres and say, "I like that. I like the stage here . . . I like the trap space here . . . I like this theatre's sightlines . . ." The difficulty is that everyone on the team also has their own agenda. The director wants the house to be intimate and the producer wants the greatest number of seats and the set designer wants more wing space. All of those issues are negotiated as we select a theatre.

Q: Can you describe the differences between working with an assistant designer on Broadway and in the regional theatre?

A: The way a designer works with a support staff is unique in both scenarios. At a regional theatre, an assistant usually provides general help. They draft, build models, and serve as the liaison between the shop and the designer. In commercial theatre, the associate designer is the most important person working on the show from the scenic end. After salaries and per diem, the most expensive part of any Broadway budget is the scenery, and the person directly in charge of that is the associate designer; they are in charge of making high-level decisions regarding technical concerns. If they're not careful and are not experienced at what they're doing, they can make three six-figure mistakes before breakfast.

One of the biggest differences in the relationship between the designer and the first assistant, or what we call the associate, is that I work for the associate designer. The associate designer is in charge of the show. For example, my associate designer, Steven Kemp, is in charge of the scenic design for the show I'm working on currently, *High*. The way the studio works within this commercial model is that I get hired to come up with the idea of the scenic design and the associate designer gets hired to make the design a reality.

To give you an idea of how this works, we will come into the studio to work together. Since the associate is in charge of the set, he will say to me, "Dave, I need you to design this, or modify that piece of scenery." And I groan and say, "OK." And I start to draw something. So in many ways, once the show gets to the theatre, I am working for them. I very much design the show, but the day-to-day activities of the studio depend on the work of those people; they're ultimately completely in charge of what goes on in the theatre.

Q: Scheduling and time lines also seem to be vastly different between Broadway and regional theatre. Using your upcoming show *High* as an example, what has that time line been like?

A: *High* has moved along relatively quickly, considering it played in three out-of-town locations. I bet we've only been working on that show for just over a year, which is a very short time frame. We went from the first phone call from the director to opening on Broadway in just over a year.

I actually won a Tony Award for a show that I designed in ten days! When I got the call to design *The Drowsy Chaperone*, it was about a two-week period from the initial call to when I had to have the show designed and off to the shops to be built. That was incredibly fast.

Now compare that to a regional theatre's schedule, where you know you are going to tech on this date, and have a dress rehearsal on that date, and open on another date. All of those dates are prescribed and given to you; whereas on Broadway, every day is an adventure! You can get a call that a big investor has pulled out at the last minute, so there's no show. Or, you suddenly find out that you don't have the theatre that you were designing for because the show that's currently in it has turned out to be a big success. You were planning on going into the St. James Theatre, but now you have to fit the show into the tiny Walter Kerr. Those kinds of crazy things come at you from all directions and are relatively commonplace.

If you happen to lose a star performer, that too can change the timeline. We've been working on Katori Hall's award-winning play *Mountaintop*, which was set to feature Halle Berry and Samuel L. Jackson for a really long time. We knew we were doing it; there were workshops; there were readings; there were different cast members considered; we even went theatre shopping here in New York. We selected the theatre we thought would be best and we were ready to get going, when suddenly the scheduling got torpedoed due to a film or another project for one of the cast members, so we had to temporarily shelve it. So, there you are, waiting to get started on something and you have to put it on hold. Then, months later, the stars (literally) come into alignment and the project is back on, and you start the process all over.

Commercial theatre is a wild, wild ride. It can be anything from getting a telephone call saying, "We want you to do this new musical and the drawings are due in two weeks," to what happened with *Thoroughly Modern Millie*: I got my very first call about that show in 1995, and we ended up doing the first version of it at La Jolla Playhouse in 2000. It can take years or it can take weeks. There's just no knowing.

Q: How does designing for the out-of-town premiere of a show that hopefully will land on Broadway affect the design?

A: Well, it can affect the design in a number of ways. The idea of developing new work, especially new musicals in the regional theatre, has certainly been around for many, many years, but it's completely taken off in the past ten years. Today, it's uncommon to do a commercial production at a rented theatre somewhere and then move it to a commercial theatre on Broadway. It's far more common to start off in the regional theatre model. When that happens, there are many things that can have an effect on the design.

Sometimes it's a show that's just being done as part of the regional theatre's season, and there's no "enhancement" money for the production; it's just part of their regular season. As a designer, you do it to the best of your abilities and if it moves on, the producers involved at the regional theatre basically have "dibs" on the future of the show if it moves on to Broadway.

The other model that's out there is that commercial producers will invest in a show that is being done at a regional theatre and they'll say, "OK. We are doing *Thoroughly Modern Millie* at the La Jolla Playhouse and we are also going to give the Playhouse [X] amount of dollars so they can make it more specific as well as offset their in-house costs." That way, La Jolla gets to produce the play and make it part of their season and get a great show. The outside commercial source saves an extraordinary amount of money this way because there's already a crew in place, there's already a theatre they don't have to rent, there's all of this in-house equipment, and there's all of this inherent capital of the regional theatre that the producers do not have to cover. It turns out to be a win-win for both the producer and the theatre.

You also could be doing it in a theatre that is physically unsuitable for handling Broadway stages. I've had shows that started out in these strangely configured rooms and those sets have somehow ended up on Broadway. The last play in the August Wilson cycle of plays was originally designed for a thrust theatre, so the difficulty with that show was that it had to go from a thrust design into a traditional, Broadway, proscenium theatre. We ended up being really fortunate in that we had had to rebuild the set for one of the latter stops on the pre-Broadway tour, which happened to be a proscenium theatre. When it finally did move to Broadway, we had an appropriate design that fit the architecture of the theatre. That doesn't always happen though. There are times when you are sitting in the audience looking at your set on opening night on Broadway and you are thinking to yourself, *I wonder if people are going to come in and wonder what all this masking is on the sides of the set.*

The regional theatre production model is here to stay, because it's been very successful. Now, when you get a call about doing a new musical, your first question is usually, "Where are we doing it? La Jolla? Seattle Rep?" That would have been unheard of many years ago, because it would have opened at the Shubert in New Haven or at the Colonial in Boston, but that's no longer the case.

Radio Golf, Cort Theatre, New York, NY, 2007
Original show drop design
Rendering by David Gallo

Finally there's the old model of designing, building, and producing it in some rented theatre somewhere as a completely commercial
venture, which isn't nearly as common here in the United States. Overseas, there's no developing new works in the regional theatre because
they don't have regional theatres. England is somewhat similar to the
US, but the projects that I do in Germany or Austria or the Netherlands are all commercial theatre ventures.

Q: How did your international career develop?

A: I had done shows at the National Theatre in London and shows in
the West End and it led me to meeting Dutch producer Joop van den
Ende, who hired me to do *Beauty and the Beast*. They wanted to do
their own European version—not the Broadway version—and tour
around the Netherlands with it, so they started the project with a new
director and all new designers. It was just something that was very interesting to me. It came at a good time, and it ended up being tremendously
successful. It's evolved, and since then we've done it in a dozen different languages. I've actually never seen this show in a language that I've
understood because it's been done in Russian, German, Italian . . .

Q: Designers are paid a fee to design a show, but are also paid a roy-
alty. Can you talk a bit about how that works?

A: When you design for commercial theatre, it's all about the long
run. The fee, the money that you are paid up front, may get you
through the experience of getting the show to opening night, but it's

not enough money to live on, and it's not enough money to keep your studio (or yourself) running either. It's all about having multiple productions and collecting royalties. Actually, if you work for years on a show and it does poorly, you'd have been better off financially if you hadn't done the show in the first place. If you work on a show that ends up being a huge success, then you are in really good shape. I have done a number of Broadway shows, but I'm still always looking for the next one to be a big hit. There have been a few designers who have designed one show and will never have to work for the rest of their lives; there's *that* much money to be made.

When you get a runaway hit, money follows. With a *monster* of a hit, designers can make pretty decent money. The earnings can get insanely high, but then that's incredibly rare. This business is all about the weekly and about having as many companies out on the road as possible; that's how you make money as a designer. I should have prefaced this entire conversation by saying that I never thought I would make any money doing this for a living. Perhaps the idea should have crossed my mind earlier, but money never mattered to me until much later in my career.

It also has a lot to do with your design remaining *your* design. That may sound strange, but what tends to happen is that the shows sort of "filter" down in scale. After the First National Tour for a Broadway show, and hopefully one more tour, a nonunion tour will go out on the road and sometimes the set you've designed that was being used will just disappear and show up somewhere with someone else's name on it. These things tend to get very complicated, and you really have to watch out for them.

To continue making money, you have to remain the designer of record on the productions you have designed. I can tell you right now, there must be a dozen productions of *Xanadu* out there without my name as the designer that look identical to the Broadway production. It's even worse when the stock and amateur rights are released on a Broadway show and there's an assumption that the scene design is included as part of the show.

Q. Is there ever a situation where you sell the rights to your design?

Sometimes you will sell the plans and design to a company. For example, there is a *Xanadu Australia* where the design that's being used is called "a design based on the original set design by David Gallo." Since they're using our design, they will pay us a small weekly royalty for as long as that show is running. That way, we just mail a packet of plans out to them and we don't have to send an associate designer.

Q: Today, can you be more selective when it comes to the shows you choose to work on, or do you still have to take every design that comes your way?

A: In order to make a living you have to continue doing what comes along. One of the advantages of being around for a while is I'm able to have a bit more flexibility; I don't have to take *every* single show that comes my way. That being said, I am a working scenic designer, and unfortunately, like any artist, we are only as great as our most recent achievement. And even if it's a play that I'm not necessarily excited about dramatically or a musical that doesn't excite me musically, I absolutely love the process.

Q: Let's talk a bit about your time at the MUNY in St. Louis. What was it like working at that huge "Summer Stock" theatre?

A: I really enjoyed working at the MUNY. It was another one of those things that happened at the right time in my career. I still remember when the producer called and said, "We'd love for you to come in and do these four musicals." I had never been to the MUNY, and if you don't know this place, it's unlike any theatre in the United States. First of all, it's outdoors and it seats 12,000 people; it is enormous! After I received some drawings of the theatre and got a description of "how it worked," I came back to my studio in New York and designed a set that they would never be able to do because I had designed it like any other design I would have created with lots of molding and dimensional scenery—something, I would later learn, that isn't done at the MUNY.

When I sent the drawings to their technical director, I got a call from him saying, "The scale is exactly right, but it's just not what we do here." And I remember saying to him, "I don't know what you mean." I had spent a lot of time on the design, and ordinarily I would have been really upset that they had wasted my time. But he said, "You just have to come out here and see this place." So I did, and I saw just how awesome and unique it was. Once I understood the concept of the MUNY, I enjoyed myself immensely.

It really is a wonderful throwback theatre. For people like us, designers, there aren't many opportunities left in the United States to work like that—it's just like 1930s Hollywood. You have a design office that looks out over the construction and paint lot, and as you draw scenery upstairs, the drawings are sent downstairs, and the next thing you know, it's built and painted by lunch! People don't believe you when you explain how it works there, but that kind of production happens within a matter of hours.

Q: Have you embraced all of the technological advancements as part of your design process?

A: As you can see, there's only one drafting table in this studio, and it's mine. That drafting table has been with me for almost twenty years. When we moved from the old studio, we went online to buy one for the new studio and discovered that it's very difficult to get a great drafting table. So we said to our studio-mates, with whom we had been friends for years, "What do you want for one of those old tables?" They said, "Just take it with you when you leave." That old piece of crap table is mine, and I still do everything on it, by hand.

Now, what was recently added to this table is a computer, so I can jump between hand drafting and drawing to this computer that has my script and research and a digital Dropbox to share files with one another. The way I work now with my assistants, who are sometimes literally all over the world, is that we just throw our work into Dropbox to share and work that way. It really works quite well.

Q: So what is your process? How do you like to begin a project?

A: I basically draw everything in pencil and in various layers—everything from initial scribbles to finished sketches, but I draw every piece of scenery for the show. Contrary to what my detractors may say, I design everything for the show. Then my sketches go to my assistant and he scans them and drafts the show from there. There was a time when the physical model was crucial in the selling of a design. Now, the work that's done using 3–D software is so much faster and cheaper. We can also render all of the transitions between scenes using a 3–D digital model to show a director exactly how the show will look. It's fabulous. The final shift has come with how we execute the painter's elevations. We're really using the computer and things like Photoshop to create our painter's elevations. I say that and now I am remembering that *Madagascar* was totally hand-painted and imported into Photoshop, so I guess we still haven't abandoned all things hand-painted. The reality is I still haven't learned those programs. I do have the ability to do open drawings?

Unfortunately, my Achilles heel is that I can only work and design sitting at that drafting table. That can be a problem because so many designers of my generation have figured out how to draft and draw on a computer while sitting on a plane or wherever they happen to be. I do have to say that it is a real liability, not being able to use Photoshop and AutoCAD with any level of proficiency. Also, for all shows that need media, like projection design, we handle it here in the studio. It used to be an added layer but it is now integrated with set design into the whole of the design. It's been a wonderful sort of fusion of the disciplines.

Q: What do you enjoy the most about working as a set designer on Broadway?

A: I enjoy the initial "figuring out" of the design, the untangling of the mysteries of the script. I believe I am very good at coming up with the design ideas, but I find some of the time in the theatre to be a bit tedious. Is it necessary? Yes. But it can also be tedious. The time in the studio is when I am energized and designing. By the time you get to the theatre, you better have figured it out.

I know some designers who don't like to spend as much time in the studio and spend more time in the theatre taking notes saying, "Let's repaint that." In my experience, that doesn't work on Broadway. If you don't have it figured out before you move into the theatre, it's just not going to happen—and if it does, it probably won't be in the way you like. I also enjoy reading the play, building the rough models, and sitting around the table with all of the collaborators. The time spent actually *creating* the design is so interesting to me. I just love that part.

If I were to make a list of my skills, high on the list would be that I have a great understanding of the score and the script. The dramaturgy of a script is very, very important to me; it's where you find the soul of the piece. Rather than doing what might be flashy or might look "cool," I think I am good at finding the tone of a piece.

I used to love to travel, but now with a two-year-old and a newborn at home, it's a bit more difficult to leave. Sometimes my family comes with me on the road, but it's still very difficult.

Q: What do you like the least?

A: What I like the least are the things that I have the least control over, and a lot of that, unfortunately, has to do with what goes on in the theatre. After you've spent up to three years of your life designing a show and you have painstakingly made sure that the elevator in the lobby of your design can accommodate six dancers and then, once the show moves into the theatre, someone decides, "Nope, I think only one person will ever go into that elevator." Then you're stuck with an elevator on stage that's the size of a semi-trailer, and there is nothing you can do to change it. That's not exactly the most fun for a designer.

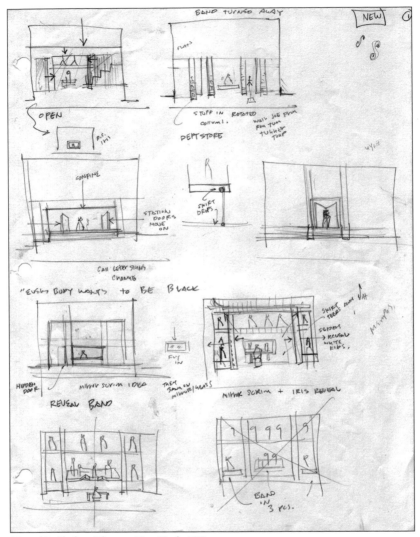

Memphis, Shubert Theatre, New York, NY, 2009
Shift scheme by David Gallo

Q: Is there a show in your portfolio that defines who you are as a designer?

A: The August Wilson plays certainly stand out, but what defines me is that there has been great diversity in my work. Others have also said that about me, so I think that is fairly accurate. I approach each

reasons to be pretty, Lyceum Theatre, New York, NY, 2009
Digital rendering, Steven C. Kemp
Set design, David Gallo

project as a new artistic opportunity; I don't necessarily have a defin-
able style. I've been working long enough now that people are able
to see my work and identify it, but that's somewhat inevitable after
twenty-plus years of designing in this city. I guess if you look at shows
like *reasons to be pretty* and *Xanadu*, they couldn't be more different.
The fun and whimsical nature of a *Xanadu* coupled with something
more austere and dark like *reasons to be pretty* is a great example of
what represents a range of style in my work.

If you look at my body of work it's a little bit more eclectic,
perhaps, than some. And that's only because it never occurred to me
that it shouldn't be. I mean, every play is different; every production is
different; why wouldn't your work be unique and different, too?

**Q: Young designers often struggle trying to figure out a director's
needs. Why are you seemingly so successful at this?**

A: I actually think I am pretty good at mind reading—getting what
I need out of a director or a playwright. I am, of course, saying that
with a great deal of humor. Early on, when I'm working with a
new director, someone I don't know at all, I just know there's going
to be this moment after we've had a couple of meetings when
someone will ask them, "How's it going working with Dave?" and
their response is probably going to be something like, "I don't

really know. He doesn't seem to actually be doing anything." It may seem that way, but what I'm doing is gathering information from them. I'm absorbing, and—as much as I hate these metaphors—"downloading" the information from them. I'm gaining their insight. So much useful information comes from the most innocuous statements they may have made during a meeting. If I can just get a director or playwright or the other designers into my studio and just talk about the piece (the way you learn to do it in college), and not get caught up with pencil and paper and a model—that's where I learn so much. Some of the most successful productions I've been involved with have come from a single statement the director or playwright made in an offhand way. The best situation happens when they say, "We could never do this, but . . ." or, "This is a really bad idea, but . . ." Usually, the "but" is: "But you are wrong. That's actually a great idea. Let's do it!"

Q: What three books would you tell a young designer that they must have on their shelf?

A: *The Dramatic Imagination* by Robert Edmond Jones is number one. I will go one step further and say that if you've gotten to the point in your life where you want to be a designer for the stage and you haven't read or memorized that book, there's something seriously wrong. *The Dramatic Imagination* is still our holy text. . . . Every time you go back to it you learn something else. That was another reason why I had a difficult time with academia—I had to find out about that book on my own. The Dalai Lama himself can go back and read a religious text and gain something new after all of his years of enlightenment, and *The Dramatic Imagination* is the same for me; it never stops giving up secrets.

> "The Dalai Lama himself can go back and read a religious text and gain something new after all of his years of enlightenment, and *The Dramatic Imagination* is the same for me; it never stops giving up secrets."

The Art of the Empire Strikes Back was, for me, really help-ful—but for someone else, perhaps not so much. I found books like *The Dramatic Imagination,* Lynn Pecktal's *Designing and Drawing for the Theatre,* and the *British Theatre Design* book by John Good-win incredibly helpful. Oh, and the Mielziner book *Designing for the Theatre,* too. You have to read that as well. I think just looking at the work of designers like Robert Edmond Jones and Mielziner is crucial, too. That was more important to me when I was just beginning than reading a bunch of books about them.

Q: What advice would you give to a young person who is considering moving to New York to pursue a career as a designer?

A: I think that despite everything that I went through, you do want to find people who will mentor you. It's the personal relationships you create that will help you succeed in this business. You've got to find people who will be receptive to, let's say, younger people coming into their established environment. I believe I am particularly receptive to new people. We've established a really strong internship program here in our studio. I've had interns who were nearly fifty years old and I've had interns who were fifteen.

We accept lots of different types of people, but one of the things we've heard from several of the interns with whom we've become very close family friends was that we were one of the only design studios in New York that returned their call and expressed an interest in meeting with them. When we get a call from someone who's showing interest in us, we usually do whatever we can to meet with her, and then possibly invite her to become part of the studio for a while. There are others who are just as accomplished and just as nice who say, "No thank you. I just don't work that way." And that's fine, too; it's really up to each individual and how they like to work. You need to find the people who are interested in talking with you.

I would also suggest that you seek out designers whose work you genuinely admire. It's very important that you know the work of the designer you are contacting. All of us in this business have varying egos, but there's nothing more disappointing than going through all of the trouble of arranging to meet with you and then finding out that you know nothing about our work; it's actually quite embarrassing. If you're going to come to meet with a designer, at least spend some time researching the work of that per-son so you can have a legitimate conversation. Hopefully you're not meeting with them because you found their name in a Playbill as the set designer. Sadly, we've had people who have done that before—with, obviously, little success.

Find people who have designed something that you enjoyed or someone who has a design philosophy you've read about that you agree with. Or find somebody whose ideas you don't fully understand but want to learn about, and contact them. Write to them—or I guess in today's world, email them—and say, "My name is so-and-so and I am really intrigued by your work on . . ."

Begin with a cover letter and keep it very simple. My name is this, and I've done this, and most of all keep it very, very brief. Also, make sure everything is spelled correctly! Even though I would have had everything misspelled, today there's no excuse. Then, contact them a short while after you send the letter and say, "I would be very interested in speaking with you." They may say, "I don't really take on interns." Or they may say, "Hey, sure. Come on over." You certainly don't want to make yourself a pest, but you need to make yourself known. There's also no need to go overboard with what you've done because, quite frankly, we don't care what you've done. We know you haven't done anything, which is why you are contacting us.

You also don't need to pad your portfolio with a bunch of meaningless filler. What's important is to let us know what it is you are interested in doing and a little bit about your background. Also, be prepared that whomever you're contacting might have suggestions for you and give you a bit of a breakdown of what you might do next or might suggest that you come in and work with them for a while or that kind of thing; you never know what direction it will take. If what you are wanting is to get yourself immersed in a studio environment, I think that's all pretty sound advice.

Understand that all of that will not help you as a designer, but it's going to help you get yourself into the world of assisting and the way this commercial business works. When a person comes to work with us here in the studio, they will quickly find themselves at tech for a Broadway show and going on scenery shop visits and, in some cases, traveling. I've brought interns to other cities and set them up in hotels with rental cars and tried to give them the whole experience of this life, depending on what it is they are doing on the project. Then, hopefully through that you will begin to meet directors, because ultimately it's through directors that we get to design. You will be meeting assistant directors, and that's the kind of connection that leads to a career as a designer—one that is based on relationships with your peer group. As a designer it's very difficult to put yourself and your talents out there. A set designer needs somebody to build his set! You need to paint it; you need to get it into the theatre; you need so much in order to just get a shot, to just get a viewing of your abilities. It is so hard. You can be the best designer in the world, but if you don't have a venue for your work, you really have nothing.

CHRISTINE JONES – SET DESIGNER
Thursday, February 10, 2011

Over the past decade, Christine Jones's life has been filled with successful professional, personal, and, most certainly, artistic ventures. During this time she accepted a teaching position at her alma mater, NYU, where she currently teaches first-year MFA candidates in theatre design. She designed the scenery for the incredibly successful Broadway musical, Spring Awakening. *She is the creator and artistic director of the critically acclaimed "Theatre for One" that was featured in Times Square in May of 2010. Most notably, in June of 2010, she walked away with a win at the 2010 Tony Awards for Best Set Design of a Broadway Musical for her extraordinary work on* American Idiot.

Christine's was a large studio with one wall completely occupied by windows. Above her desk was a large collage of photos and drawings in what could have been considered a haphazard arrangement; however, upon further inspection, it was clearly a "designed" collection of images that were set in a careful and deliberate assemblage of tone, color, energy, and mood, telling a story all by themselves. A conference table, where we would conduct our interview, occupied the center of the room.

She quickly hung up our coats and warmly greeted one of her assistant designers who happened to be cutting out model pieces for an upcoming project. "That's Jon," she said. "He is wonderful—you really should be interviewing him as well. The assistant designers here in New York are incredible."

Q: Were you eager to move to New York and attend graduate school?

A: When I moved from Montreal, Canada, to New York to attend NYU, I did so with great excitement. About nine months after I graduated from NYU, I panicked and moved back to Montreal for a short spell. I then renewed my courage and returned to New York, determined to weather the uncertainty. Over the course of the following eight years I built a career and a life. I was in a long-term relationship. We shared a dog, a loft apartment, and a country house, but I was designing thirteen or fourteen shows a year and traveling a lot. The relationship ended and my life changed dramatically. I moved into a tiny apartment with a friend who was a costume designer, and a year later into another apartment with my new boyfriend and three other guys, including the playwright Adam Rapp. My rent went down to $300 a month, so I chose to do fewer shows. I found I was able to put more passion and energy into each project and relished the ability to become more invested in each individual process. My work got better, and I fell deeper in love with being a theatre maker.

A good way to deal with the uncertainty is to keep your living costs as low as possible, or find a part-time job that helps pay the bills. One of my current assistants keeps his job at Lincoln Center because it pays well and has flexible hours. In my case, it has been teaching that has helped supplement my income.

Q: Did you always have aspirations to be a Broadway set designer?

A: I never ever thought I would be doing Broadway shows. That notion was so *not* where I thought I was headed—not when I came to New York as a student, not once I graduated, and not even when I began working. I never had Broadway in my vision, but I am grateful that I have had the opportunity to work on a larger scale with incredible people. It's the dream-I-never-had come true.

Q: How important is it to understand the business of design as well as the art of design in order to have a successful career in the theatre?

A: Important. When I graduated from NYU with my Master of Fine Arts, I remember feeling quite overwhelmed to suddenly discover that not only was I a designer, but I was also running a small business. The experience of studying design is different from the daily practice of living as a designer. You learn so much when you are at school, but it's hard for schools to convey all of the business information relating to taxes and assistants, in addition to drawing and concept building. I do think it is important to be aware that business and art go hand in hand. As a teacher—I teach the first-year MFA candidates at NYU—I try to bring some of those discussions into the classroom at moments that feel appropriate. I think that assisting is one of the best ways to observe a designer in full action. Eavesdropping on conversations a designer is having in the studio with their agent or producer can be edifying, and I have always found my mentors happy to consult when approached.

Q: What are some of the tough questions a young designer should ask himself before embarking on a career in design?

A: I think things you have to ask yourself are questions like: Am I comfortable with being freelance? Will I be fine with not knowing—month-to-month or year-to-year—what my income is going to be? Am I the kind of person who likes to travel and find myself in strange towns where I don't know anybody right away and am thrown into weird theatre housing, or do I really need my home? What is the quality of life that you want? That's not necessarily what you will achieve the first few years out of school, but I think it's good to outline the direction you want to be headed in. You need to be okay with the scenic route, which might take you on some muddy back roads, and you might get lost, but it's pretty along the way. If you are the kind of person who needs to take the high-way and stick to the map, you may want to explore other options.

Q: How long should a young person who is thinking about moving to New York expect it to take to find their niche?

A: I tell people that I think it takes at least four years after you've graduated from school to find your groove. When I graduated, I was very, very fortunate and had some lucky breaks, but even with those lucky breaks it took a few years to find the community of people, or what I like to call the "tribe" of people, that I was probably going to work with for years to come. One job leads to another, you meet new directors, you assist someone new, you get a call out of the blue, and then eventually people and places fall into patterns and you have found a niche, at least for a while. The great thing is it keeps evolving, and you keep meeting more amazing people along the way.

Q: What advice would you give someone who is considering moving to New York to start his or her career?

A: I still think the first question you have to ask yourself is, What kind of lifestyle do you ultimately want while you work? I definitely think that if you have a desire to live in New York City, you shouldn't be afraid of it. People often talk themselves out of taking risks, and risk taking is absolutely a part of this process. Never be afraid to risk. I've never seen anyone come here and not have an apartment or food to eat. I've seen some move away from theatre after a while because they

"I definitely think that if you have a desire to live in New York City, you shouldn't be afraid of it. People often talk themselves out of taking risks, and risk taking is absolutely a part of this process."

find something else that they like better, but everyone's situation will be unique. You may find yourself working as an assistant designer while designing smaller shows off-off-Broadway, or you may find a job doing something else entirely while still working in the theatre.

I tell my first-year graduate students when they come up to their first summer, if they can find a way to make some income in retail or the restaurant business and work with a designer as an intern, even for one day a week, it's a great way to meet people. It's a great way to get a window into what the life of a designer is really all about. To see the day-to-day realities can be incredibly valuable.

In my first year out of school, even with the designs at the Public and at Hartford Stage, I still had a waitressing job on the weekends. I worked Saturdays and Sundays at a tiny little restaurant where I made great tips. I was lucky to have a very inexpensive apartment, which was also a financial lifesaver. Two days a week waitressing covered most of my rent and basic living expenses, so I didn't need the income from assisting as much. If you can keep your living expenses down it gives you more options. As you assist part time, you will have time to take on designs of your own, even if they are for no money at tiny theatres.

There are so many different ways to have a life in the theatre, and for every person, the picture is going to be unique. Some people are going to live in New York and work off-Broadway theatre, some people are going to do mostly regional theatre, and others still go on to do both. Some people will do opera, television, film, or event design. Some will travel a great deal and some won't travel much at all. Some will go into teaching. My advice is to start by looking inward and thinking about what you want your home and work life to look like. Slowly but surely, you can design your life, just as you would a play. And similarly, it starts with a concept, and the best one comes from the heart.

Q: The life of a theatre designer is not really that of someone who has a job; it's really a lifestyle. How do you relate that concept to your students?

A: I tell my students that every day I am more grateful for what I get to do for a living. Once you start to find your "tribe"—or the community of people that you love making theatre with—it just gets better and better. Sometimes work, play, and life are indistinguishable, especially since your collaborators become like family. The most important thing is to find the people you want to spend your days with, no matter what kind of work you are doing.

You can choose what your lifestyle is like. You can make choices that allow you to have more fun, or make more money. I had a teacher

On a Clear Day You Can See Forever, St. James Theatre, New York, NY, 2011
Directed by Michael Mayer
Lighting, Kevin Adams
Costumes, Catherine Zuber
Scenery, Christine Jones
Production photo by Michael J. Riha

who said, "Say yes to every job," but I don't subscribe to that philosophy. Take the job that doesn't pay if it is something that you really want
to do. Don't take the job that pays well if you don't want to do it. You
don't have to say yes to everything. Lowell Detweiler, a brilliant professor
at NYU who teaches painting and drawing and history of costume and
décor, said, "There are three criteria you should look at with each job,
and it must fulfill two of the three: fun, fortune, or fame. The job either
needs to pay well and be a lot of fun, or it needs to pay well and be not so
fun but good for your career, or be fun and good for your future, but pay
nothing. I've often used that formula to make decisions.

**Q: When did you find that the workload was too great for one person
and realize that you were going to have to hire an assistant?**

A: In the first year after graduating, I was hired to do *Tartuffe* at
Hartford Stage with Mark Lamos and *Texts for Nothing* with Joe
Chaikin at the Public. Having those two shows as my first professional experiences was crazy fortunate and unexpected. However, they
were scheduled to open right around the same time, and suddenly
I needed to hire an assistant because I wasn't a fast draftsperson or
model builder and they were main stage shows happening quickly.

I didn't feel comfortable asking the people I had just been at school with, so I asked someone who had graduated a year before me if they could recommend someone. I hired their recommendation and muddled my way through, but then I went back to doing everything myself for the next few shows. The workload ebbs and flows, and with that so does the need for assistants.

I did feel awkward wondering how much I should pay an assistant. Theatres often don't have assistant budgets. As a designer, you're not paid by the hour, you're paid a flat fee for the entire design, but assistants often get paid by the hour. (It is often much more lucrative to be an assistant!) If you pay them by the hour, however, chances are that the fee, if there is a budget for one, will not cover the number of hours required. Over time I've gotten more comfortable asking people if they will work for the assistant's fee, just as I work for a design fee, but it has taken me a while. When I first started to hire assistants, I felt terrible not paying them hourly, so I would pay "out of pocket." Jon Collins, who recently assisted me on *The Illusion* at the Signature Theatre, said to me when he heard I was doing the show, "I love the director, I love the play, I love the playwright and that theatre. If you need someone, I am your man, and I will do it for the fee." He knew he would work many more hours than he was going to be paid for, but for him it was an investment he was happy to make.

Q: When a young person comes to New York and starts as an intern or an assistant, does she have to join the Union in order to work in the city?

A: Most certainly she does not. That being said, even if she chooses not to join the Union right away, she will need to develop the same skills as Union designers. If your goal is to work on Broadway shows, you do have to join, but there are plenty of shows that are not Broadway shows you can work on. If your skills are such that you can get into the Union and you can manage the dues, you can join right away. You will make more money on Union shows and maybe qualify for healthcare; but it's not necessary to join right away—especially if you don't feel your skill set is up to par. Take time to work on bolstering your drafting and other skills so you have a better shot at getting in on your first attempt.

Q: If a student gets out of a graduate program in design and still needs to bolster their skills, do you see that as a problem with the training or just part of the reality of what there is to learn?

A: I look at it this way: It's just the way it is. So much of it has to do with how proficient you are with the computer and how proficient you are doing computer drafting, Photoshop, and those kinds of renderings. Some people grew up attached to a computer, and others are encountering some of that for the first time in undergraduate school or even in their graduate training. Some of the first-year MFA designers come from backgrounds where they may not have had any theatre training. Those students will probably need more time after school to get themselves up to the level of "hirable."

When you're looking to hire assistants, you recognize what their strengths and weaknesses are. My assistant Jon will readily admit that he doesn't love model building as much as he enjoys drafting, so I'm more likely to hire him to do the drafting and hire somebody else to do the model building. If you can focus on at least one thing and do it really well, with the understanding that you will work on the other skills in the time to come, that's a fine way to proceed. This means you have to be honest with yourself about what still needs work. Teachers and designers with whom you interview will be straightforward with you and say, "It was great meeting you, but I'm looking at your drafting and it's not yet at the level where I can personally hire you to draft; however, I might be able to hire you to do model building." I do think it is advantageous if you can make yourself available for internships. Many of the assistants I work with started as interns.

Q: There is so much to learn about this profession and the only place to learn that is on the job—and sometimes that will mean having to work for free.

A: Yes, exactly. If you didn't get into this for the money, then keep the money and the art separate for as long as you can. If part of the reason you got into this was for the money, then go for it and do everything and anything you can: film, television, event design. There are certainly ways to focus your energies to get more lucrative work; but in the beginning, no matter what your long-term goal is, working for free as an intern or as a production assistant is an invaluable way to learn on the job, and to make great connections. Most of my assistants came to me through interning, eventually got paid, and have forged long-term relationships with me. When I began to work less, my associate Ed Coco began working at MTV doing event planning. He continues to work full time for MTV while he drafts my Broadway shows on the side. This keeps him in the theatre world but provides him with a steady paycheck.

Q: How many assistants do you tend to keep on your staff?

A: My "staff" is small and fluctuates between one and three people at any given time. I consider myself a part-time designer. I have created a "triangle": I mother, I design, and I teach. I work in my studio two days a week, teach one day a week, and am a hands-on mom the rest of the week. I try to create an equal balance. Sometimes I will go so far as to create a diagram and count the number of hours I am being a mom as opposed to designing or teaching.

Compartmentalizing is something that I've become good at, and it's a vital skill. I also think you get better at it as you go. For me, it began by juggling multiple projects, and then it moved into juggling multiple aspects of my life along with those projects. In the beginning, your family often takes a backseat because that's the window of time in which you are investing your time and energy into building professional relationships. Eventually those relationships take root and you can spend more time with friends and family and nurturing other aspects of your life. I'm constantly planning out how I am going to spend my time and trying to adhere to the triangle plan as effectively as I can. My triangle often turns into an octagon, but at least I have a template.

Q: What about your current staff of assistant designers? Who are you currently working with on a regular basis?

A: Evan Alexander and Ed Coco are the two people that I've had the longest relationships with. Both went to schools that necessitated they do an internship. Somehow, they figured out a way to come to New York and live for two or three months, during which time they offered their services to me full time. After they both graduated, they decided to move back to New York and came to work for me. Evan worked for me for about seven years and Ed's been working with me for at least the last six years, probably more. I am deeply, deeply indebted to both of them.

Jon Collins came to me already living in New York City. At the time, he had a job at Lincoln Center doing archival work and was making a pretty good salary doing it, which allowed him to offer his services as an intern to me. When he first began, his skills were rudimentary at best. He started doing research and a little bit of model making and drafting, but not a lot. He had been to an undergraduate program but had a lot to learn. He worked one or two days a week for three years and eventually was accepted into NYU, where he was my student. When he graduated, we picked up where we left off and I've been able to hire him on more and more sophisticated projects, recently as an associate designer who supervised load in and tech for *Everyday Rapture* on Broadway, which was suddenly remounted while I was in previews for *American Idiot*. When I handed Jon *Everyday Rapture* to tech and load in because I was too busy, he got to be in the hot seat with a great director and a fabulous writer at a well-respected theatre. He's also nurturing relationships with young directors, people he met at school, and people he's met since. I think he's finding a way to handle both assisting as well as establishing himself as a designer. It can be done, with faith and patience.

Q: Is there a fear of being pigeonholed as a lifetime assistant if you do that for too long?

A: It depends. It is a risk. But it is a risk that goes both ways. When I first graduated, I assisted Tony Walton briefly for a few weeks on the theatre his daughter was opening in Sag Harbor. A lot of the work I did wasn't so much drafting and model building, but rather helping him get into the new theatre space and get the first show on its feet. What I did learn from Tony—which was incredibly valuable—was hearing him on the phone with producers and directors and watching how he dealt with his assistants and seeing how kind and generous he was with them. We all came to his studio in the morning and Gen, his wife, made breakfast for us and we would all have lunch together. I learned a lot about how welcoming he was with his assistants.

The period after graduating is when you get a chance to fine-tune your skills, and it's a little like learning a foreign language. You study the language in school but when you get to France, you realize, wow, I actually don't know how to speak French. But then you live in France for three months and you become fluent. It's a little bit the same with theatre design. You're drafting and model building in school, and you're really learning, but you aren't necessarily 100 percent fluent until you get out and start working. I've always felt that my drafting and model-building skills were never fully realized because I didn't do more consistent, rigorous assistant work after school. I have no regrets, but I've experienced a reluctance to work with moving scenery or more complicated structures as a result of this lack of mastery.

To go back to your original question, yes, there is the risk that if you start your career assisting, you could find yourself only assisting. And there's also the risk that it will get harder to take the financial hit that comes with being the designer after you get used to an assistant's wages. But I think there is a way to balance the risks with the benefits.

Q: One of the more practical components of being a designer is "bidding" a job. Do you have any sage advice for a young designer who is faced with that task if they have never done it before?

A: Never hesitate to call other more experienced designers and ask their advice. Work hard to meet deadlines so that the bidding process has time in which to happen, and so that revisions can be made in an organic fashion. Also, meeting deadlines shows the people working with you that you respect their needs. Showing respect makes it easier to ask for more time or money when you need it. I subscribe to the idea that working within the given circumstances of time and money is wise. If you design a $50,000 set that has a $5,000 budget, it's going to be painful for everyone, and the design will suffer. Find out in the beginning if the budget is $500 or $5,000 and whether or not that includes the labor. Then, forget about the budget and design the show with the sense of scale that that number gives you, until someone says, "When."

If it is a Broadway or union-built show, never be at a bid session without a producer present. If money is being discussed, the money people should be there. If you have never worked with a union shop and it is a big show, try to get an assistant or, better yet, an associate, who has more experience than you.

Q: How did the *Spring Awakening* project find its way to your studio?

A: Luck played a huge role in my landing *Spring Awakening*. In 2005, my boyfriend Dallas Roberts, who's an actor, was working with Michael Mayer on a film and we got to spend some time together on location. When Michael was asked to direct *Spring Awakening* off-Broadway at The Atlantic Theater, he asked me if I would be interested in designing it with him. We crossed paths at NYU, but had never worked together. I never even showed him my portfolio, but he must have seen some of my work over the years and had a gut instinct that I might be a good choice. Michael has an astonishing, encyclopedic memory, so if he had seen my work, he would have remembered it. This was one of those "fun" and "fame" combinations—certainly not "fortune." The pay was low, but it was an opportunity to work with someone I was intrigued by, on a musical based on a play that I loved. It was Michael's vision and serendipity that took the show to Broadway. Then the pay got better and all three "ƒs" were fulfilled in the end—fame, fortune, and fun!

Q: Using *Spring Awakening* as an example, did the budget for the set inform or influence what the show was going to end up looking like?

A: No. The overall design was influenced by the unique space of The Atlantic, which is a converted church. There we were, working on a piece that was set in a society repressed by religious and social norms, and the raw shell of a church was also our theatre. It was a gift.

Top: Production photo, Doug Hamilton
Spring Awakening, Eugene O'Neill Theatre, New York, NY, 2006
Directed by Michael Mayer
Lighting, Kevin Adams
Costumes, Susan Hilferty
Set, Christine Jones
Bottom: Design Collage for musical number, "Purple Summer"

Q: When I saw *Spring Awakening* on Broadway at the Eugene O'Neill Theatre, I was struck by the set and how it seemed to evoke a wonderful quality not unlike that of a dance environment. Was dance ever a part of your life?

A: It's interesting that you say that, because you have those moments where you look back at points of genesis. For me there were two moments that helped set my course: One was when I was ten years old and I saw *The Turning Point*, which is a dance film with Anne Bancroft and Shirley MacLaine. I came home and sat on the dishwasher and cried to my mom, "I have to be a dancer! I have to be a dancer!" I did study dance quite seriously, but when I realized that the lifestyle of a dancer was not one I was prepared to commit to for my entire life, I started to do more theatre.

While I was at Concordia, I saw a production by a company called Carbon 14. It was a French company with a director named Gilles Maheu and they were doing a production called *Le Dortoir*. It was about a dormitory and featured a visceral combination of dance and design. I remember one scene in which they had metal beds that were spinning around the room and performers were diving under them and over them—that was the second genesis moment for me. When the play ended and the lights went down, I was in the house, weeping, knowing that was the kind of work that I wanted to do. It was the physical, kinetic, interactive electricity between the furniture elements and the room and the people that got to me.

When I came to New York, the desire to do that kind of work was what fueled me. But it wasn't until twenty years later when I was designing *Spring Awakening* and especially *American Idiot* that I felt like I had reached that goal. When I met the choreographer for *American Idiot*, I mentioned the production *Le Dortoir* and he said, "I've seen that film." It was one of the first films that inspired him to be a performer, too. It was a beacon for him as well, so we instantly had a common vocabulary with which to talk about *American Idiot*. One of my favorite moments in *American Idiot* is when they tip the scaffolding down and turn it into a bus. That moment alone is like, "That's it!" That's what I was after—*that* moment. I like to create spaces that have physical potential.

Q: Are you a designer who attends the first table readings?

A: That is my favorite part, except I always think afterwards, "Darn it. Now I have to ruin it!" Those moments in the rehearsal room when it's just the words and the performer in an empty space and you're only five feet away from the performer are the best. I love those moments, and I try to keep those moments present in my designs. I'm doing everything I can with the physical environment to maintain some aspect of that intimacy and immediacy. More often than not, I haven't done much work on the design, so I'm able to allow the reading to really influence the direction I'll go in.

Q: There seems to be some divided opinions about the word "networking." What is your take on this divisive word for such an important part of becoming a working designer?

A: It's funny because it is sort of a "bad word." People often ask me, "Does your agent get you jobs?" and my reaction is, "Oh, no, absolutely not!" A part of me would be mortified if my agent was calling people and asking them if they wanted to hire me. I have many discussions with my agent about what jobs to take and how to juggle everything and get the support I need, and he does all the contract work. Any hour he spends reading my contract is an hour I can spend designing or with my family. The 10 percent commission buys me time. As for "networking," I don't think there is anything wrong if there is a designer or director whose work you admire to write them a letter saying, "You are somebody whose work I really admire. I would love to have a chance to show you my portfolio and would be grateful for your feedback." Due to the busy schedules of most theatre artists, it's often difficult for them to make time, but if there's a sincere appreciation for someone's work, it should be acted upon.

I prefer to think of "networking" as finding your "tribe" or your community, so I think going to a lot of theatre really helps, so you can identify what kind of people you want to work with doing what kind of theatre. I spent time working as an usher at BAM so that I could see a lot of shows. If you are going to PS-122 or Second Stage,

> **"I prefer to think of 'networking' as finding your 'tribe' or your community, so I think going to a lot of theatre really helps so you can identify what kind of people you want to work with doing what kind of theatre."**

you're starting to get a feel for what type of work really excites you. Which directors excite you? Instead of this blanket idea of networking the vast industry, first think about what it is that "turns you on" about theatre. Then start going to those types of shows. Familiarize yourself with what that particular company or director is doing, and then maybe you offer yourself as an intern.

Networking should be creating relationships based on your very specific passions. Instead of looking at it as, "Well, I need to get a job," it's actually that you are figuring out your life. If your passion is for "revenge tragedy," write a letter to Jesse Berger and say, "I am a whore for revenge tragedy and love your work." That is flattering to just about anyone. Jon, my assistant, is assisting on every show at the Signature this season not only because it is great work for him, but also because he believes in the theatre's mission and the quality of their work. You could say he is "networking," or you could call his investment in working for a fee and his attendance at opening and alumni nights "nurturing new relationships."

Q: Are you ever faced with the fear of the blank canvas where you may feel like you have run out of ideas? What do you turn to as a safety net to get creatively motivated again?

A: One of the things I teach first and foremost is to find a way to fall in love with the play you are working on. I've written a list that is titled "Seven Ways to Fall in Love with a Play." If you are honestly getting intimate with that play, you can avoid the blank canvas or empty model box. I think one way to do it is to keep reading, keep researching, and keep sketching. It is easy to become paralyzed.

The process of design is a physical manifestation of emotional and intellectual impulses. You must be *physically* engaged as well as mentally and emotionally. You are literally creating a three-dimensional environment that people will walk in and around. You have to build that to fully understand it. Sitting at your table thinking about the design isn't going to get you there. You have to be drawing, you have to be modeling, you have to be making collages, and you have to be reading. You must be physically active. Make notes; make a list. You have to physically engage

"The process of design is a physical manifestation of emotional and intellectual impulses."

with the work. For me, the physical realization part starts with writing words on a page. Those words become images, then the images become model pieces, and then the model pieces become built scenic pieces.

That said, I also think that if you can turn the blank-canvas moments into silent prayer, there is value in silence. It's within silence, when you can be asking yourself questions about the play, that the play might start speaking back to you. I often use time on the subway to reflect on the play without actively trying to "work" on it—that, for me, is quite useful. Also, asking myself, which of these characters do I most easily respond to? or, Is there any kind of experience I've had in my own life that this play brings up for me? Mostly, it's important to put the panic aside and figure out what the next action you can take will be—make a list, reread the play, start a model, or go book browsing, and learn to let the stillness be active, too.

Q: The long hours, the travel, and the unfortunate need to eat food we may normally never eat due to convenience, takes its toll on our bodies. How do you approach your health as a working designer?

A: I do the best I can and celebrate the small triumphs. If you expect too much of yourself it's easy to fail, so I try to set reasonable goals. With two children, teaching, designing, and being artistic director for Theatre for One, I have little time left for myself, but I do what I can. I do yoga once a week. It's not three times a week, but once a week, for one hour, and it makes a huge difference. It's like anything; I believe baby steps will eventually get you where you want to go.

For example, Theatre for One is something I've been working on for ten years and it's taken me a long time to turn it into the physical manifestation of my original idea, but each little step along the way moved me much closer to where it is today. That same approach can—and should—apply to diet, exercise, and sleep as well. Baby steps.

Q: Theatre for One is your brainchild. Can you talk a bit about this unique approach to live entertainment?

A: I had recently attended a wedding where a magician performed a magic effect for me in a very intimate way. I was so overcome by the experience of magic and how moving it was to experience something normally witnessed publicly so privately. I got into theatre because I love going to a show and being undone; I am a junkie for that feeling. I began to think about how I could get that pure form of the drug. Theatre For One began as an experiment: What happens if you take everything away and you put the audience and the actor in an incredibly intimate setting?

When you are starting off in this industry, it is easy to be dissuaded because you may say, "Well, I have this degree and all of these ideas. Now, who is going to hire me?" You have to remember, it's not the theatre's job to figure it out for you—it is your responsibility to make the kind of life and the kind of work that you want to make. Theatre for One has been a lot about that notion. There were certain kinds of things that I wanted to explore and so I just started to do it. I love it when I see people start their own theatre company. Who knows if that company will sustain itself, but regardless, artists are feeding themselves and not just waiting for the job you've always been waiting for to show up on your doorstep.

Theatre for One came about because I wanted to design a church. I was thinking about how a theatre is a kind of sacred space and I thought it would be beautiful to design a church. But then I thought, "Nobody is going to hire me to design a church. I'm not an architect, and I'm not religious." So then I had the thought that, well, if I made a church for one, I could build it myself. As much as I love the collaborative work that we do as theatre designers, sometimes it's important to be the "first heart" and set off the first sparks, the initial impulses in creating a project. I had read something that was put out by the New York Theatre Workshop. They had issued a call to artists announcing that they were doing a series of laboratories and were inviting people to submit proposals. I thought, *Well, I should come up with something.* And I thought, what if I made a Theatre for One instead of a Church for One. And then I started taking the necessary baby steps.

Q: Do you find that you change your process depending on the type of show you are designing?

A: I would say my process is my process, but there are different elements I mix and match and reinvent sometimes. I don't treat a play any differently than a musical or an opera. I will investigate the words. I will listen to the music. If there is no music, I will make my own playlist. I will draw. I will collage. I have my own kind of "dance routines" that I put myself through. In an ideal situation, I get to do some of everything—text work, listen to music, create collages, drawing, etc. Sometimes it may be that I have a condensed amount of time so I don't get to do as many of the parts of the process as I would like, but the more process work that I do, the less likely I am to come across the "empty black box" paralysis we talked about. I believe in the idea of "front loading" your time and your effort on your internalization of the play. I think sometimes we get afraid and so we rush to design too soon. I encourage my students to hold off on designing until after you've fallen in love with the play work—courtship before marriage.

Theatre for One, Times Square, New York, NY, 2010
Artistic director and creator, Christine Jones
Photo courtesy of Doug Hamilton

Q: Do you share all of your preliminary work with a director, or is that private?

A: It really depends on the director. Sometimes they aren't interested in it, but most of the time I share it with them. We usually meet at my studio, and I will often have a collage and/or drawings up on the wall with images that pertain to a model we are working on, so the process work is there and around to refer to as we go. Lately, developing *On a Clear Day You Can See Forever* with Michael Mayer, we have been literally ripping images off the wall and putting them into the model as we go through scene by scene. My goal is to have used every image I pinned up on the wall in some way, somewhere in the design.

Q: What are the differences between collaborating in an academic setting and the professional world?

A: I think one of the hardest things that I had to learn was timing—when was it the right time to talk to somebody about ideas, changes, etc.? I came out so fired-up and excited about things that sometimes I was trying to share ideas when it wasn't quite the right moment to do so. When you are a student, you are so often in critique and discussion mode that you talk freely all the time. In the professional world, you need to carve out the right moments to engage in collaborative discussions. You're responsible for building a supportive atmosphere that is challenging and respectful, and for considering where the other people are in their process when things need to be questioned. There have been times when a director is in the middle of staging something, and I find myself tapping them on the shoulder and asking, "Is that really what we want to do here?" That's not the time to have that conversation.

In school, discussion and critique are always welcome, at least in my experience; however, outside of school, some directors want you to be a collaborator in certain areas but not in others. Being able to take their temperature or being able to read that particular director is an invaluable skill to develop—and that takes time. There are some shows where I'm very much involved with the staging and the direction and there are some shows where I'm not, and that's fine, too. I've come to really be OK with both situations.

Q: How do you like to express your initial ideas for a design? Is it through sketch modeling or is it by just drawing the ideas as a thumbnail?

A: Initially I like to do a lot of work with just the words—the text. I like to go through a kind of distillation process where I pull out words and phrases that become touchstones or ideas that I can keep coming back to. Then I usually like to collage using the research I have gathered. I also enjoy doing charcoal drawings. I usually don't get to a model until I've done a lot of other things first. Honestly, I do rough, and I mean very, very rough model work and

American Idiot, St. James Theatre, New York, NY, 2010
Design collage, Christine Jones

then work closely with my assistants. I am very lucky to have that kind of help.

Q: When you build a model, do you begin with a white model first or is it complete with color when you show it to a director?

A: I believe that it is important to flesh out ideas of shape and color at the same time and to make them as alive and true to life for the director as you can. You need to make sure that your painted model, or your research, or whatever it is you are sharing with them is as accurate and specific as possible. It's really important to be sure that you've shown them everything and that you're not just talking about ideas; that you are backing up your words and ideas with visual support that is accurate and accumulative.

Q: It sounds as if color is not a separate entity in your process; rather, it is integral at all stages of the design process. Do you tend to move right into color or do you work with white models?

A: I was taught that you always work in color—everything happens simultaneously. This belief is handed down to me from the Oliver Smith and John Conklin schools of thought. Oliver Smith would have painted a color rendering before a model was completed, and John wouldn't be caught alive or dead with a model that wasn't in color. The emphasis is on everything happening at the same time. The model is a colored, three-dimensional sketch. One should aspire to rough out color models that evolve as opposed to creating pristine white models that get a coat of paint. The idea is that you want to have to explain as little as possible—which is why, I believe, having the color on the model is preferable to a white model.

Q: As you came up through the ranks, did you ever feel like your being a female designer, in what has historically been predominantly a "boy's club," hampered your ability to succeed?

A: Only once when I made the transition from working with non-union shops to an all-union shop, and in that case it was probably more my inexperience than it was being female that hampered me. I actually feel being a woman often works more to my advantage than as a disadvantage. I've almost always felt that to be true—I could be wrong, but that's what I feel. Not knowing women in the field who were also having kids did make me wonder if I could do both: be a theatre designer *and* have a family.

When I graduated I knew of Adrienne Lobel, Heidi [Ettinger] Landesman, and Marjorie Kellogg, but I had never met any of them. I had no idea what their lives were like. My teachers were all men: John Conklin, Oliver Smith, Campbell Baird, Fred Voepel, Lloyd Burlingame, and Lowell Detweiler. Patricia Woodbridge taught me drafting but she was a film designer.

I began reading biographies of Georgia O'Keefe, who had no children, and of Diane Arbus, who struggled tragically with being an artist and a mother, and I really didn't know if it was possible to be a professional theatre artist who also raised a family. I'm proud that I have had a number of young women come to me and say, "You are my role model because I see that you have a partner and children and a successful career and it's so great to see that it can be done."

Many of the theatres I've worked in embrace the fact that I do have a family, and directors are very supportive as well. I tend to choose projects where I know that kind of attitude prevails. There are always exceptions. Somebody once asked me to interview with them and I knew that he had a family. His assistant called me and asked if I could meet with him at 6:00 AM on a Saturday morning, and my response was, "Absolutely not." I can't imagine working with someone who even suggests that we have a meeting at 6:00 AM on a Saturday morning. That's insane!

Q: Is it strange to have won a Tony Award when you never thought you would design on Broadway?

A: It is absolutely incredible! Recently, I brought my Tony to work with me in a bag because I had never gotten it engraved. When you win a Tony, you're supposed to give it back to them to get it engraved right away, and ten months later I still had not done it! When I got to the office, my intern was joking and asked, "Can I take a picture of myself with this and send it to my parents?" And I said, "Absolutely!" She did and attached a note that said, "Mom and Dad. I'm in New York. Things are going really, really well!" We all got a good laugh out of that! Now it is at home, on my shelf, engraved. It's a year later and I still get "I-can't-believe-it" butterflies in my stomach every time I see it.

Q: How does it happen that the shows you get land on your desk and not on another designer's?

A: Again, it's the relationships. I know that sounds like a broken record, but that is truly what it's about. You work with a director, you hit it off, and that director invites you to work again. Or you're friends with a costume designer and they recommend your name to somebody, or the director will recommend your name to another director friend of theirs. It's a series of coincidences and random en-counters, and it boils down to relationship building, not networking. Also, I know a lot of excellent cocktail lounges in New York City, and I love to play card and dice games when I'm out of town. I think that might have something to do with why I get calls, too.

Q: If you could recommend three books that should be on every de-signer's shelf, what would they be?

A: My first-year designers' reading list has on it Rainer Maria Rilke's *Let-ters to a Young Poet*, so that would be one. A second would probably be a biography of a personal favorite artist. One of my favorites is *Sculpting in Time* by Andrej Tarkovsky. He was a filmmaker, and I respond to the way he writes about his process. The book I give all of my friends is Anne Carson's *Autobiography of Red*. It is about a boy who is a red monster—inspired by an ancient Greek character named Geryon—and how he grows up to be a photographer.

One has to give oneself permission to be an artist. Reading about the maps other artists followed can help you gain the courage to follow your path. It took me a while to get the courage to call myself a designer and now, instead of referring to myself as a designer, I like to call myself a theatre artist, if I'm feeling brave. I'm still working on the ability to call myself the artistic director of Theatre for One. It feels strange to say, but it's pretty much the truth.

It takes courage to *own* a title, but once you do it can help you to move forward with confidence. More important than the "how-to" books are the ones that will inspire you to find your path, and help you have faith that it will reveal itself as you go. When I came to New York, I thought I was landing on Mars. I didn't know anybody who went from my undergraduate program in Montreal to New York; for that matter, I didn't know anyone who had graduated and left for the United States! It felt like it was a giant leap into the great unknown.

Q: For all of the designers who are studying in Arkansas, or Idaho, or Wisconsin, and really want to pursue a career in this field, what words of encouragement would you like to give them?

A: If it's what you want to do, you absolutely can do it. There is no way to predict what your life will look like, but trust that there is a way for you to have a life in the theatre. There are many ways for you to have a life in the theatre. Believe, and take chances. I don't have a savings account and I'm way behind in starting a pension, but I love what I do, and I love the people I do it with. When I head to the studio in the mornings I tell my kids, "I'm going on a play date." And that is the truth.

ANNA LOUIZOS – SET DESIGNER
Wednesday, February 9, 2011

Ms. Louizos might be considered a "new kid on the block" as far as Broadway designers are concerned, even though she has been in New York designing scenery since the early 1990s. She began her career working as an assistant designer for Broadway greats such as Heidi Ettinger, Adrianne Lobel, and Tony Walton, but her big break came in 2003 when she designed the off-Broadway hit Avenue Q. The show began its life at the Vineyard Theatre at 108 East 15th Street, where she garnered a Lucille Lortel nomination for Outstanding Scenic Design. Since then, the show has had a successful run on Broadway and has recently returned to its off-Broadway roots. She remarked, "That show just keeps going and going. It continues to blaze new trails."

Like many who chose theatre, Anna Louizos grew up with aspirations of one day becoming a Broadway performer, not a designer. Somewhere along the way, however, that path was diverted and she was led to seek out what was being created backstage. As a young girl growing up in California, Anna's interest in design may have blossomed during the many afternoons she would spend helping her father with building projects and repairing Volkswagen Beetles in their garage. Her father, a schoolteacher by trade, would rebuild VW engines for extra money for the family. When I asked her about where she got her talent and creative mind, she quickly attributed it to her father. "He taught me to think about how things work," she said.

Q: Did you grow up in a family that attended plays and musicals on a regular basis?

A: Actually, my dad was a high school teacher and my mother worked in a medical clinic. We would go see the occasional play or musical, but my family was not involved in the arts professionally. My father taught me a lot of things because he was very good with his hands, and I was always his assistant. He was also an amateur Volkswagen repairman—that was his hobby and I got to be his mechanical assistant. He was a very creative person, and helping him when I was growing up definitely helped foster my interest in building and creating things. We also traveled through Europe several times and lived in Greece for a year, where I experienced a great deal of cultures and places. My mother loved musicals and would take us to San Francisco to see Broadway tour productions, which opened my eyes to the theatre.

Q: What was the artistic and theatrical path that led you to your current success like?

A: When I was in high school, my first impulse was to be on stage, so I wanted to find a school where I could train as an actor. I got accepted into Mills College, a liberal arts women's college in Oakland, California. I attended for two years, and I performed in many productions, but the program wasn't very extensive; eventually I transferred my junior year to NYU, which had an undergraduate drama department affiliated with a number of professional acting schools. I took studio classes at Circle in the Square Theatre School.

Throughout my high school and undergrad years, I was also interested in what took place backstage, so I'd help hang the lights, build the sets—and even while I was at Mills, I took a set design course. I remember that my teacher was quite encouraging with me because he thought I had ability and said I should really think about doing something in the technical or design area. At the time I said, "No, I really want to be on stage." Then, you come to New York and you are a tiny fish in a huge pond.

After graduating from NYU School of the Arts, during that summer, a group of my friends and I put on a show. One of them produced it, one of them directed it, one wrote it; I built the sets and another person lit it. This experience gave me a taste of what designing would be like, and I gradually decided to shift my focus. After spending the next year waitressing I decided to focus my attention and career path on design. The following fall, I applied to the graduate program in set design at NYU and was accepted. Since I was financially unable to attend full time, I was allowed to attend part time with the stipulation that I would switch to full time the next year. During my first year of graduate school I took foundation courses in drafting, drawing, and model making. I learned the skills, but I also felt that after only one year, spending that kind of money to learn a "foundation" wasn't the best choice for me. I needed to see what it was really like to actually design in the "real world."

After my first year, I left and spent the next five years assisting. It was during that five-year period that I really learned the business of theatre; that was my training. I was able to see, from the ground up, how scenery was constructed by going to the shops, meeting with people, and seeing how things worked on stage. I was also able to assist some really great people on a number of plays and musicals.

My skills were actually pretty good at the time because I could always draw, and attending NYU for that one year really helped me to focus my abilities toward theatre design. I was living in the East Village at the time, waitressing to make money, but looking for ways to get work as an assistant. My brother, who also lived in the neighborhood, mentioned that he knew someone who was a set designer and told him about me. So I introduced myself and got my first assisting job with the late designer John Falabella. Over several years I worked as his assistant/associate on and off, and we eventually shared a studio together.

During that five-year period I worked for other designers like Doug Stein and Adrienne Lobel, working primarily as a model builder. It was at this point that I realized that I could either work as an assistant forever, or I give myself a chance to develop as a designer. At the age of twenty-nine, I decided to reapply to NYU and went back to begin the MFA program in design. Even though I had completed a few credit hours at the graduate level, I started over completely and did the full three-year program.

Q: What was it like to virtually start over in the MFA program after five years of professional experience?

A: It was fine, actually, because I now felt that I had established roots in New York. This was my home; I could afford my East Village apartment; my restaurant career had turned into a managerial position, so I was able to pay my rent and support myself while I was going to graduate school. That was very important at the time. Also, NYU was only three blocks away from my apartment, so it all worked out very well.

When I returned to graduate school, I returned with very clear-cut goals. I wanted to get into the United Scenic Artists Union because, up to that point, I had always gotten the nonunion position in the design studios. Back then, you still had to take an exam to get into the union. So, after completing the MFA program, I took the exam, got into the union, and went right back into the world of theatre design. I was still assisting mostly, but now, since I was in the union, I was a better-paid assistant!

Q: What type of work did you find after you graduated with your MFA?

My first job out of graduate school was working as an assistant art director in television on *The Cosby Show* for one season, drafting the sets for each episode and supervising the set construction and live videotaping. I also began to design occasionally for little off-Broadway shows. I was using my skills in a number of ways—now, just on a different level. Through connections with former classmates and colleagues, I was able to get the occasional television or film job, in New York or on-location for a few weeks at a time.

The jobs usually involved drafting sets either for shooting locations or soundstages.

Q: Do you remember how you got your first break as a designer, where you knew you were on your way to establishing yourself?

A: Yes. I designed a production of *Tick, Tick . . . Boom!*, which was kind of a prequel to *Rent*. It was based on a solo show that Larson had written and performed a few times under different titles. After he died and *Rent* went on to become a huge hit, there was renewed interest in reviving some version of his solo show. Victoria Leacock, one of Jonathan's close friends, and a group of producers explored ways to consolidate all the multi-titled versions of Larson's solo piece. Robyn Goodman, one of the producers, enlisted the playwright David Auburn to take all these disparate versions and put them together to create a cohesive script that is now an ensemble piece called *Tick, Tick . . . Boom!* It was my first time working with Scott Schwartz, the director, and it was the beginning of a very long and successful association.

Q: Many designers who move to New York will have to begin their career as an assistant. What advice would you give them as they seek out this kind of work?

A: Well, now it is even easier than it was back when I was getting started, because anyone can create a website for their work; everyone has access to email, and it's fairly easy to find people's addresses, so you can send designers with whom you may want to work your information and design experiences long before you have to meet them face to face. You no longer have to print out an expensive physical portfolio of work to mail to the designers, which saves you money as well as time. Now you can email images of your work or send a link to your website—but an introductory letter is also very helpful. In that letter you can include a reference to your website portfolio. Also, don't be afraid to follow up, because if you don't hear back from a designer, like me for example, it's not that I want to be rude or that I'm not interested at all in people's work, but rather that I am busy and I get a lot of emails. Sometimes I will read them with the intention of getting right back to them, and I—unfortunately—forget. If a person reminds you and makes it easy for you to have some contact with them, I think it helps. So, I guess what I am saying is, don't be intimidated or shy. It's better not to be shy and show designers that you have skills. That too is very important, especially if you want to work as an assistant. The more skills you have, the better the chance you will have of securing work.

Q: When you are looking to hire assistants, do you tend to look for a person who has especially strong skills in one area in particular, or a range of talents in many skill sets?

A: I do tend to look for specific skill sets, but everyone in my office tries to do everything, because right now we are so busy that we are bouncing from one project to another. So sometimes a person might be drafting on one project but might also be building a model on another. It's great when you can just concentrate on one thing; maybe one person will end up working on a model because they are in the zone. But since it's a team effort, it helps when people have the ability to jump from one skill to another. It's challenging, but if you have more skills, then it offers more opportunities for you to work for someone in a number of capacities.

Q: How long has your current staff of assistants been with you?

A: Some have worked for me since 2001 and some have arrived in the last two or three years. One of my assistants, Donyale Werle, was a former student whom I taught drafting at NYU. She started with me on *Avenue Q* and then worked on *White Christmas*, *High Fidelity*, and *In the Heights*, and now is designing on her own. Her designs for *Bloody, Bloody Andrew Jackson* garnered a Tony Award nomination.

    One of my assistants, Jeremy Foil, sent an email saying he was interested in meeting me. We set up an interview and eventually I brought him in on a production of *Minsky's* in Los Angeles. He now works for me, but he goes back and forth between his own work and assisting me. Others here work on their own projects, too, so I try to give them the time they need; but they're welcome back whenever I have work.

    I met Michael Carnahan at the Williamstown Theatre Festival in 2005 while I was doing a play there. At that time, he was their resident designer and helped coordinate the out-of-town designers hired to do projects. When I was about to do the musical *Curtains* on Broadway, I thought of Michael because he was living in New York and he had expressed interest in working with me. So I hired him, and we have worked together on and off ever since.

Q: There's a collaborative component that is unique to the theatre world, as opposed to being a fine artist. Was that something that drew you to this field?

A: Yes, that is huge. That sense of collaboration is what makes it exciting and interesting. I think more so than being a writer or a painter,

Top: Production photo, Anna Louizos Studio
Avenue Q, John Golden Theatre, New York, NY, 2003
Directed by Jason Moore
Lighting, Howell Binkley
Set, Anna Louizos
Bottom: Set rendering, Anna Louizos

where you are somewhat forced to sit in a room by yourself, I really thrive on the conversation and on hearing one idea spark another. Currently, we are working on a new production of *Aladdin* for Seattle's 5th Avenue Theatre. There are multiple scenes in the marketplace, which need to have movement, so we created some rough quarter-inch scale units for the model that would allow Casey Nicholaw [the director] and me to play with in our early discussions, moving them around in different configurations; this gives a scale representation of what we could actually do on stage. One idea builds on another and allows us to find a way into the piece. What is ultimately created and realized on stage is the result of that collaboration.

Q: As a student, collaboration seems less complicated, in the sense that all design members are usually sitting around a table working together to create a unified vision for a production. In the freelance world of Broadway, does that happen?

A: In this day and age it's tough coordinating everyone's schedules, often because people are working on other shows. Meetings can be challenging, at least in the early stages, but when it comes to anything that has to do with how the show moves, or how the story gets told, I very much want to be a part of that conversation.

A lot of times, if the director and the writer are together in the room, I like to know what they talk about because sometimes it affects me directly. Sometimes, in the storytelling, the playwright doesn't necessarily have the capacity to see how to get from one scene to another.

There are so many varied levels of skilled playwrights out there today, especially with younger playwrights who don't necessarily have a theatre background. A good number of playwrights are writing in a style that seems to demand a more cinematic approach; however, you don't have to necessarily accept that how it's written is the only way to do it. Sometimes you need to have a conversation with the playwright and the director to address the practical issues of getting from one scene to another. It can be incredibly helpful in the collaboration to explain concerns with the playwright and to give the playwright some room to start to think of alternative ways to flesh out a story.

That's what I think is so wonderful about the collaboration part of this process—no one is able to solve the problems alone; everything has to be brought to the table, and I don't feel like, if it's written this way, that's the only way to do it. Just like I don't feel like, if I design it this way, this is the only way it can be designed. I know there are many, many ways to design something. I've discovered that when someone says, "This is the way I see it, and I don't see it any other way, and as an artist, I cannot compromise"—I think that's not the truth. I really think there are many ways to do something. Take for example Shakespeare, where you have endless possibilities.

Q: Do you have a process or formula for designing that you utilize for each show, or does your process change show to show?

A: I think it depends on the show. What I like to start with is just some time to let the show "percolate" for a while. I don't like to have to rush into the designing part right away. It is during that "percolating" time that something will just pop into my head for one reason or another due to how I respond to the piece. Usually, I don't even know if it's a real idea, but I do my best to try to trust those early impulses. It's important to trust your first impressions. Even if they eventually get thrown out, I try to go along and see where those ideas lead me.

I usually try to compile images and visual material that somehow speak to me about the piece. I will also start to scribble some stage pictures that I have in my head, which might relate to some ideas that have come to me through what I've heard in the score or read in the script. Then, even if they don't relate to one another, I try to find what it is about those separate pieces that might serve as threads to tie them together. What's also important is how the whole piece works together. There needs to be some relationship—either through the production's design style, or color, or something else—that ties it all together.

Another critical design aspect is movement—how you get from one stage picture to another. To me, that's critical. As the designer, if you haven't figured out how to get from one picture to another, you haven't done your job. I believe strongly that, as designers, we are responsible for figuring out how to take the audience from one scene to another as fluidly as possible, and if we don't, we've failed. Now, that doesn't mean I have to have all of the answers, but it means that I have to talk to the director and say, "I can't figure out how to get from here to there. We need to address this." Then the director can say, "Perhaps I can stage something where we can do this." I think that kind of communication is vital to the collaborative process. If the director doesn't have an answer, then you have to figure out how to make it work. If you wait until tech when you are sitting in the theatre, and you have this great big scene on stage and the next scene has to be completely different and you haven't figured out how to get

"It's important to trust your first impressions. Even if they eventually get thrown out, I try to go along and see where those ideas lead me."

there, you are doomed. If the audience has to sit there watching things get pushed off and it's not part of what's been staged, then that's a failure on the part of the designer.

I think you are asking a lot of an audience member if you've created a style within a piece that is breezy and light and goes from one scene to another smoothly, and then suddenly there is a scene where the audience is seeing scenery move in a way that has never happened before and is not in the "language" of the play that you have created up to that point. It will draw focus to that moment, making it look like a mistake. If, however, you establish the "language" of the piece—where, for example, scenery flies in and out throughout the show—the shifts will appear integrated. If an audience suddenly sees a rock wall fly out after not having seen any set pieces fly, you are changing that language and style within the confines of which the audience accepts your conventions. Ultimately, it will appear as if the designer did not do his or her homework.

Walter Bobbie [the director for *High Fidelity*] and I spent a lot of time talking about the scene changes in *High Fidelity*. He really set the bar early as to how he saw the story unfolding from the protagonist's perspective. He wanted it to seem like the leading man, this slacker of a guy, was basically saying, "This is my life, and this is what happens to me, and here is my record store and this is my bedroom, etc." Walter wanted the set changes to spring out of the lead character and appear to happen all around him. He also said the set should look like a bunch of smart "slacker guys" just threw this thing together; like they literally pulled it together to make the record store happen. For me, this meant the set had to have the texture and feel of the world that these people lived in, which made it pretty tricky.

Q: Were you forced to change the look of the scenery in order to make it work within the framework of the scenic shifts?

A: Yes, and in addition to that, the script was changing and evolving while we were designing it. Sometimes, when you have a new piece and it is written one way and you are struggling to get it to work, being able to change the script can help you.

For example, we started off with one scene that was going to first take place in a nail salon. Then, we changed it to a restaurant, and finally it was a deli. We explored multiple locations in which to set one particular conversation. When we previewed in Boston, we decided to set it in an "in-one" scene that was designed to look like a deli, but because it was restricting the space too much, due to a fairly large R & B number with choreography, we ultimately decided to set

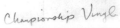

Top: Pencil sketch, record shop set, Anna Louizos
High Fidelity, Imperial Theatre, New York, NY, 2006
Directed by Walter Bobbie
Lighting, Ken Billington
Set, Anna Louizos
Bottom: Production photo, Anna Louizos Studio

it back in one of the main settings, the record store—and it worked just fine. That was an example of a time when we spent the money, made it look the way we wanted, and then we just cut it. That happens more often than you might think.

Q: How can production budgets affect your design choices?

For *Avenue Q*, the director, Jason Moore, and I began by discussing how to integrate the world of the puppet characters with the humans on stage, so scale became a primary concern: whether the puppeteers should be visible or not, and how to represent the living spaces of the puppets and the humans. The show was going to be presented at the Vineyard Theatre, a small off-Broadway venue, and when Jason and I presented our concept to the off-Broadway producers, initially the scope of our design was much too grand for their budget. Our idea for *Avenue Q* was to have revolving buildings and flying scenic pieces. Their response was, "We can't afford that; you're going to have to rethink it." So then we said, "Damn, OK. So, let's just rethink it." So we went back to the drawing board, pared it down, and simplified it. We decided to embrace the simple, flat, presentational style and use the set as a modified advent calendar with some built-in surprises. Once again, that's an example of a design you can do many, many ways, and all of them can be right. I always think the end result is better when you are given parameters. It helps me get to what's really important and is essential to the storytelling and the style of the piece. And I think, ultimately, it made the show better.

Q: Regarding the design you created for *In the Heights*, talk a bit about the layered effect you created with the overlapping scrim facades. How did you arrive at this unique design for such an identifiable location as Washington Heights?

A: Tommy Kail [the director] wanted to create a sense that there were more people on the set than there actually were due to the limited size of the cast. Also, he wanted it to feel as though there were many layers of streets and buildings, and the way I knew how to do that was to use scrim for surfaces of the buildings. Our first production was off-Broadway—another example of a show that transferred to Broadway—so I got to experiment. I started by using painted scrim for the walls to cover the steel-frame outlines of the buildings. I figured it would be the best way to see through the buildings and still evoke the architecture, and to highlight the most interesting parts of those buildings, which were the detailed moldings and trim. The skeletal elements of the buildings identified the prewar look of that architecture, and since the brick itself is nothing exciting to look at, it just seemed like the best way to handle it.

There were also physical requirements. We needed height and we needed to create the sense that the buildings were multi-storied. People needed to be on fire escapes, so the structures had to support their weight. Because we were limited by the height in the theatre, we had to create the illusion of more height than was realistically possible. To achieve this, we changed the perspective and the scale of the architecture, so the windows got smaller the higher up you went to create a stronger impression of height.

Q: Is there one particular part of the design process that you enjoy more than others? Is it the research, sketching, model making, drafting, or is it tech week?

A: I love it when I feel like we've found the right "language" and everything starts to fall into place. And certainly when the final model is finished it's exciting because you know what the show's going to look like. It's pretty amazing how when it's on stage, it really does look like the model—without the lighting of course—but it's pretty exciting when you look up on stage and say, "Wow, that was in my head five months ago!" That's very rewarding. It's also very rewarding for my assistants because they contribute a great deal. It's the collective troubleshooting that's so great about having skilled assistants. They think like designers, because they're all designers in their own right; they're not just working for me. And since we've worked together so much, they also know how I think and know what I look for.

It's also important for me as a designer to make the actor feel safe. And to think about their safety while I'm designing is crucial. I'm not an engineer, I'm not saying that, but I need to design something that makes them feel safe on stage—that's very, very important to me. I also like to provide actors with an environment that they feel really works for the play and their characters. I always try to picture what it would be like to be on stage as I am designing, mainly because they will have to be on it for hours at a time. I think it's just another part of my job to make them feel like this is where their character lives.

Q: Do you have a specific place where you like to do your creative work?

A: Well, for one, I do not work at home. I like to keep them separate; otherwise the work would overwhelm my private life. When I go to my studio it puts me in the right frame of mind. I also find creative time when I travel on a plane, train, car, or subway; it helps me focus on whatever design I happen to be working on at the time. Sometimes, early in the morning, when I'm in a half-dream/half-awake state, between 5:00 and 7:00 AM, it can be a great time to think about a particular aspect of a design, and this often helps me solve design problems. Having a workspace that is well set up makes it easier to do research, sketch ideas, and build models. Focusing on design while I am here is exciting to me.

Q: Do you ever feel like you are running out of ideas, and if so, where do you turn for inspiration?

A: What really works for me is to talk to other people about whatever the issues are. Talking to the director; throwing my hands up in the air saying, "I can't figure this out. I don't know what to do." I also talk to my assistants. I may also seek out other directors to talk to them as well. If I am struggling with a director, I will ask another director for advice as to how to improve our communication. And, if I still am not getting the information I need, all I can do is cover my bases and make sure that whatever I put on stage is something I can live with. I don't ever want to feel like I've either given up too much or that I am embarrassed to see what I've created.

Q: What do you do to make sure that you take care of yourself physically as well as emotionally?

A: Diet and exercise are very important to me, but sometimes I can get too preoccupied with work and let things slide. It's also funny that when I am out of town I seem to take better care of myself than when I am home in New York. I actually have time in the mornings to go to the gym every day because I am focusing on one thing and I'm not distracted by having to walk the dog, or get up and feed the cats, or take care of other business matters. Part of it is, I feel guilty if I don't get to the studio early enough. This means that sometimes I have to forego the gym. I am, however, walking back and forth between the studio and my apartment, which is a twenty-block walk that provides me with some exercise on a daily basis. What's also great about being here in the studio is having a kitchen. We often eat together—and it's generally something healthy—which creates a communal feel within the studio.

Q: When deadlines approach, does that seem to motivate you or negatively affect your creativity?

Time management is a skill I have learned over the years, and I think I've gotten much better at it than I used to be. Having people work on projects with me affords me peace of mind, so that I don't have to hold all the cards myself and I can distribute some of the responsibilities. If all I have information-wise is the date of our first preview and when we load into the theatre, then I back up from there and say, "OK, the shop's going to need this many weeks to build it, and this many weeks to look at the drawings to figure out if they can build it for the set budget we have, and then prior to that, this is my design time." This is how I time-manage each project. I try to impose my own deadlines in order to keep myself, as well as the staff, from going insane.

Q: How did you maneuver your way through the business side of this career?

A: When I started, I would work for free. I mean, I was so grateful to be doing it that I'd work for free, or for very little money. Whatever designer I was working for, he or she would have a limited amount of money for their assistants. It's usually either up to the designer to pay the assistant out of his or her own pocket beyond what the allocated assistant funds might be for a show, or the assistant accepts the work and the limited fee without regard for the hours. In my case, there were times when I was paid only $400 as assistant designer and I would work for three full weeks on that money. Ultimately I didn't care, because I had a restaurant job that paid my bills. I did it because I knew I was learning something; I was learning a skill and knew that I had to absorb as much as I could, so I just counted it as experience.

Having gone through that, and being in the place I am now, I constantly have to fight to get more money for my assistants. Either my agent or I will go directly to the producer and say that there's no way I can do this project on the current amount. Even when they give me additional assistant money, it's never enough. I usually end up paying some portion of my assistants' pay out of my own pocket. I actually have a payroll system in place, which distributes paychecks and the appropriate paperwork. It's crazy how underpaid people are in this business considering the amount of work involved.

Q: Do you enjoy it, creatively, when you are asked to work on plays that seem to have prescribed scenic requirements?

A: Actually, yes; they can be a lot of fun. I don't always get a chance to do them, but *Arsenic and Old Lace* was one of those projects for me. That's an old chestnut, and I was able to work with a wonderful director, Scott Schwartz.

Scott wanted to give *Arsenic and Old Lace* a fresh take. Because the stage of the Dallas Theatre Center [housed in the Frank Lloyd Wright-designed Kalita Humphreys Theater from 1959 to 2009] had a turntable that covered the entire stage, we decided to play

Top: Production photo, Anna Louizos Studio
Arsenic and Old Lace, Kalita Humphreys Theatre, Dallas Theatre Center, Dallas,
TX, 2011
Directed by Scott Schwartz
Lighting, Jeff Croiter
Costumes, William Ivey Long
Sets, Anna Louizos
Bottom: White Model, Anna Louizos Studio

with the idea of seeing more than just the interior of the house, which is traditionally how it is mounted. We decided to stage the entire top of the show outside of the house, and we added a scene that isn't even written in the play. In our new opening scene, you see a dollhouse sitting on a box in front of the darkened house. The music suddenly builds to a climax and the dollhouse explodes. The brother, Teddy, then comes out of the house wearing his gas mask and carrying a TNT detonator. He stops, picks up some of the exploded pieces of the dollhouse, and proceeds to walk back into the house through the porch as the entire house starts to revolve to reveal the interior.

As this is happening, you first hear the sound of an organ playing, and as the house revolves to the interior one of the sisters is seen playing the organ, singing a hymn with the priest from next door. During the entire opening scene there's not a single word spoken, but what we were able to do is establish the tone of the play. This all came from a conversation that Scott and I had very early on in our discussion of the play.

Q: What role do you play, during tech, when it comes to discussing ideas with other designers? How do you make your concerns known without overstepping your boundaries?

A: There have been a few times when I've had to say something to a lighting designer. I do like to give the lighting designer some time, because the poor lighting designers have their time squeezed into only the time that they are in the theatre. Now, because a lot of the shows have moving lights, they can change things quite easily, but time is still very short. For instance, I try to allow them time to set the scene, but if we come back to that scene a few times and it still looks a certain way, depending on who the lighting designer is, I will approach the designer to ask them about it. Some of them I feel very close to, and I can go up to them and say, "Howell [Binkley], why is it like that?" And Howell will say, "Well, that's what the director asked me to do." However, if I don't have that type of relationship with the lighting designer, I will talk to the director first and say, "Why is it so orange? I feel like it's killing the color on stage." Sometimes I can give them a reason, like the colors I chose for the wall are supposed to evoke a certain feel or atmosphere and when the color that's being used on the walls is killing the color, it's actually detrimental. And then, the director will say, "Oh, I didn't notice that. OK, I will talk to him and say something." The conversations really depend on the relationship you have with either the lighting designer or the director, and that's something you have to figure out as you go along.

Q: Since designers and directors have such limited time together in the theatre, what advice would you give a young designer in order to create a collaborative and productive environment?

A: The thing to remember (and I often need to remind myself of this, too) is that when we are in the early stages of design, lighting should be part of that discussion. Casey Nicholaw and I were just talking about that very issue with *Aladdin*. Natasha Katz is the lighting designer, and Casey urged both of us to start talking early, because we're going to try to do a simpler, graphic version of this play's design. Even though it's a Disney piece, it's being licensed through the Seattle 5th Avenue Theatre, so their budget is smaller than what one might think for this type of production. As a result, we will rely on the lighting to help us change the atmosphere, as well as take scenic pieces that can be broken up and reassembled into different combinations to tell us [the audience] that we are now in a different place. So in this case we will be talking very early on in the process about how lighting can help achieve that.

Of course, I show the lighting designer the model and give them the drawings; then we negotiate lighting positions (in the ground plan), and sometimes that requires adjustments. With certain people I've worked with over the years, we've established a kind of "shorthand." I try to think ahead about where I may have certain surfaces in the units but not much room in the air where we want to light these surfaces. I then build something into the scenery to help the lighting designer achieve that, which always makes them happy—the more lights, the better! More lighting equipment really affords more opportunities to cover every possible surface with light, and that provides the director with more options as well, so it's a good thing. When a director asks, "Can you put more light over there?" the lighting designer's answer can be, "Why, yes, I can!"

Q: Do you find meetings with directors without the other designers in attendance beneficial, or should all of the design members be present whenever any design ideas are being discussed?

A: I think initially the first meetings with the director are usually conceptual, about the big idea, the overall theme and feel of the piece, so it generally is about the environment, the world in which the play exists. It might be helpful to include the other designers, but I often find it more beneficial after the director and I have come up with the look and feel of the piece first. Sometimes, you may be with a director who doesn't quite see the play the same way you do, or doesn't have a strong opinion about the lighting, so it might be more productive if you go to the lighting designer with your ideas. If the director says, "Yes, it doesn't bother me if you want to talk with the lighting designer without me," then it's fine. But in reality, most directors like to be part of the decision-making.

Q: Do you run into any challenges as a female in this industry?

A: I think, when I was younger, the fact that I was a female was more of an issue. When I was going into the shops for the first time or working as an assistant, I didn't have the ultimate responsibility of the designer, who happened to be male, so they took the lead role and I was just a support person. When I was finally able to take the lead role, I felt like I had enough experience under my belt and that I actually knew quite a bit. It's important to know what you're talking about and to be able to anticipate the problems or the issues that might come up so that you have an answer and are prepared.

Also, the way I think about design is not just about the pretty pictures; it's how it works and how it functions that interests me. Therefore, I don't rely on the technical people to tell me how things work. I tend to suggest to them how I'd like it to work, and then we have a conversation about it to refine my idea. Like I said earlier, I think my obligation is to figure out how the scenery flows—even if I don't know the actual mechanics; I want to know how it's going to affect the look of the design. I truly am interested in how things move and what technology is used to automate pieces. It keeps me up to date on what is out there, and maybe that has given me some degree of credibility with the shops and crews.

I actually think we are at a different point in history, too. Twenty years ago, I don't think there were many women in design. I think what's been happening recently is that the trend has shifted.

Q: Are there certain qualities, aside from the obvious technical and design skills, you would advise young designers to keep in mind as they enter this business?

A: When you get started it's important to remain as positive as you can, have a willingness to adapt, and to not be reactive. Take it all in, be proactive, and solve the problem. I'd say in general the prevailing atmosphere and emotional attitude of everyone who works in my studio is one of calmness. Being calm, steady, and laid back, yet not too easy-going, actually helps to keep everyone very focused. The assistants who work in my studio are incredibly focused and they're easy to get along with. I think, as human beings and creative people, we all have a tendency to easily slip into that frenetic mode, which can quickly become problematic. Here, since we are all tuned in to the atmosphere we are creating in the studio, and because we take in a lot from those around us, we all tend to respond to that calm balance, which allows us to be creative. I prefer people who can be proactive and who stay even-tempered. It seems to me that artists tend to be sensitive to their environments and more in tune with taking in the emotional temperature of a room.

I think, whether it's your childhood upbringing or whatever it is that brought you to that place, it seems that a lot of creative people come from similar circumstances. This is a *huge* generalization, but I think creative people often grow up in difficult or unstable environments. Creative people tend to be very aware of what is going on around them, so if you create an environment that is tense and unstable, people tend to react to that by either withdrawing or emulating that behavior. But if you create an atmosphere where everyone stays calm and steady, it allows a person to breathe and focus on the *work* rather than on someone who is acting like a crazy person. And that energy starts at the top. If I can stay calm, everyone else seems to be able to stay calm.

Q: Are there resources you seek out for information and inspiration that may not be affiliated with theatre?

A: I love music. I listen to a lot of music. I also like to read. I'm reading historical books right now. I'm in a book club and we are currently reading about all of the presidents. We've started with George Washington and we will eventually have read a book about every single president. We figure that in about ten years we will be done! I love it, because it gives me a new perspective on American history, and a timeline, president by president, of how this country evolved politically, economically, and geographically, and how interconnected it all is. It's one of the non-theatre things that I am enjoying quite a bit. I also try to keep current with events—what's going on politically and throughout the world.

Q: Is there one book that you would tell all young designers they should have on their shelves?

A: *Architectural Graphic Standards* is actually a very good book, the kind of book that tells you things like: When you build a table it needs to be "this" tall. There are several editions of this book, and some of the earlier editions that have hand-drawn illustrations that are wonderful.

Q: Do you think, had you attended graduate school somewhere outside of New York, you would have ended up in New York doing what you are doing now?

A: No. I probably would not be in New York, but I don't think being from New York or having attended Yale or NYU is a prerequisite, either. Three of my current assistants all came from outside of New York and not one of them came here with a secured job; they just came to New York with a little money in their pockets. I met Hilary, one of my current assistants, when I was at Joe Forbes's Scenic Art Studios. I was looking at some muslin drops that were being painted, and she happened to be there on that particular day because Joe had told her to come by to see the shop. While I was there, I met her and Joe said, "This young person is recently out of graduate school and is looking for work, maybe you can hire her sometime." I said to her, "Call my studio so we can meet." That's how it happened. She came, showed me her portfolio, and I told her I thought I might be able to hire her for a little bit of work. Then, about a couple of weeks later, I had some work for her and I hired her.

   Another assistant of mine, Aimee, who is a friend of Hilary's, came to New York for a vacation and came to the studio with Hillary one day. Aimee had some free time so I put her to work cutting out some model pieces while she was there. After that brief visit, she returned to her home. She soon decided to move back to New York, so I hired her soon after she moved here.

Q: Do you have any advice for young people who want to begin to establish their careers as designers?

A: I learned that a lot of it is being able to distinguish yourself from others, because there are so many people wanting to do this. You need to create your own design identity. Another important factor is timing. Being in a place where there is a need for you and your skills—you know, being at the right place at the right time. It's not

> **"I learned that a lot of it is being able to distinguish yourself from others because there are so many people wanting to do this. You need to create your own design identity."**

necessarily a reflection on you being the only person who can do this job, because there are plenty of skilled people. A lot of it is just timing. Also, building relationships with other people in this industry—that's what's critical to your success.

I would advise young designers to associate themselves with directors as soon as they possibly can. If there is a director at college that you meet, build that relationship. Try to build an association and friendship and working relationship with directors, because that's how you get jobs; it's the only way you get jobs as a designer. You see these people, directors and designers, who have worked together for years and years. These collaborations have gone on for decades because they started off at the beginning together and they've grown together. I thought that if I worked as an assistant for years and years that somebody would hand me a job; unfortunately, it just doesn't work that way. Designers don't give other designers jobs. It can happen, but it's not the direct path.

As for trying to find your way into this business, I'd say if you see a play that you really like, seek out that director and let him or her know. Say, "I really liked what you did with this play and I would love to work with you sometime," or, "If you are interested in working with other designers, I'd love to work with you." But make sure you see their work so you have something to talk to them about. It is really flattering to a director when they know that you've seen their work and you can see the kind of approach that director takes in that particular piece of theatre. It will also let you know if it's the kind of work you'd like to be involved in.

Q: Any final advice for young designers regarding the pressure of this industry?

A: The process and the result of what we do in the theatre have to be put in perspective. So few of us get to do this for a living, considering how many people out there want to do this. It's a privilege to work on a show and create something that people are going to pay money to come and look at and enjoy, so yes, I believe we are very, very lucky. We have to remember that, when there are moments where we are stressing out about this and that, we still need to enjoy the process. If we didn't have a job as a designer, what would we be doing? I try to keep that in mind.

It's also really important to eat your meals, take a nap, and do the things you have to do to stay healthy and clear-headed. I, unfortunately, have to remind myself of those things because I get so involved with what I am doing. Generally, we do not work past 6:30 PM. When

"*The Underpants*"

Top: Set rendering, Anna Louizos
The Underpants, The Alley Theatre, Houston, TX, 2005
Directed by Scott Schwartz
Lighting, Pat Collins
Costumes, David Woolard
Set, Anna Louizos
Bottom: Production photo, Anna Louizos Studio

the clock hits 6:30 PM, we go home. When it gets to that point, I say, "Go home guys. There's always tomorrow." We all get to the studio at 9:30 in the morning, and we don't work weekends. I try very hard to keep some semblance of a normal work schedule, because if I didn't, artists would work all of the time. When I was younger, I would do that all the time. I'd stay up all night, working; in graduate school I was up all night doing my projects. But not anymore. It's very important to keep this all in perspective and to enjoy what you do. Of course when you're starting out I think it's probably necessary to push harder, so you can distinguish yourself.

Also, keeping a sense of humor is very important. Part of what I have learned—and what makes this business so wonderful—is the importance of the relationships with the other people involved. I have to remind myself when things are getting crazy that we're not saving lives here. It's not an emergency ward; it's just theatre—we're just putting on a show.

DEREK MCLANE – SET DESIGNER
Thursday, May 19, 2011

Between 1996 and 2011, Derek McLane received over thirty-five nominations for his set designs at off-Broadway, Broadway, and regional theatres across the country. In 2009, he won the Tony Award for Moisés Kaufman's 33 Variations *and, most recently, in 2011, the Drama Desk Award for the revival of Cole Porter's classic musical* Anything Goes. *To say that Derek's designs are in "high demand" would be an understatement. At one point during the spring and summer of 2011, Derek was in the process of opening three shows on Broadway, including* How to Succeed in Business Without Really Trying, Anything Goes, *and* Bengal Tiger at the Bagdad Zoo. *In addition to his commitment to three Broadway productions, he was also working on four off-Broadway shows:* Blood from a Stone, Marie and Bruce, One Arm, *and* Death Takes a Holiday. *In addition to those seven shows in New York City, Derek's work was featured at the Kennedy Center's revival of James Goldman and Stephen Sondheim's 1971 musical,* Follies, *starring Bernadette Peters. Opening eight productions in five and a half months, three of which occurred within a ten-day window, is an achievement very few could handle.*

Q: **When you were growing up, did you see a lot of theatre?**

A: No. My parents were both professors. I grew up in Evanston, Illinois, and my mother has always been very interested in the arts. She took me to a reasonable amount of theatre in Chicago when I was a child, but I certainly didn't imagine this is what I would go into as an adult. I certainly didn't act in shows when I was a child, nor did I participate in them during my high school years. I really stumbled into it while I was in college.

Q: **When did you become interested in set design?**

A: While I was an undergraduate at Harvard, I was asked to help build a show because I had some modest carpentry skills that I had learned from building houses. So, I'm an undergrad, and I've agreed to help build this show, but I'm totally clueless as to how to go about it. It was a production of *Guys and Dolls*. While we were working on the show I remember thinking, *I have to do this*. I was hooked from that moment on. So, with absolutely no skills, I went on to design a lot of undergraduate productions at Harvard. There wasn't a theatre program at Harvard. I was an English major; however, the experience was still great in a lot of ways. I got to meet a lot of really interesting people and design a lot of productions while I was there.

Q: Since you grew up in Illinois, when you left for Harvard, was it difficult for you to be so far from home?

A: I was actually ready to leave Chicago. I had gone away to boarding school for two years before I went to college, so I had already experienced leaving home. I love my parents, and I love the town of Evanston, but I was definitely ready to go somewhere else. Plus I had always imagined that I would move to New York. The minute I moved here, I thought to myself, *Yep, this was where I was meant to be.*

Q: How do you think your English degree has enriched your work as a designer?

A: Well, theatre is text-based. We all start with the story; we are storytellers. As designers, we have to read the story first and then figure out how to tell that story visually. However, underneath that, we need to find the "tone" of the story, what that tone is, then translate that into the set. Being able to understand how the story feels and being able to incorporate that into the set design is very much related to my English degree.

Q: Did you take a lot of art classes while you were an undergrad?

A: I had a few. I didn't particularly like the art department at Harvard because it was very academically oriented. I was required to take an art class—Classical Drawing I. Everyone was required to take that before being allowed to take any other art classes. Classical Drawing I literally taught students how to draw squares, circles, and triangles, and I just thought, *This is not what I am looking for at all.* Drawing is about *seeing* and they just didn't offer a course like that. I went to the head of the Art Department—twice—to see if I could get out of taking the class. I basically explained that I could already draw these basic things; but they refused to let me skip the class. At that point, I ended up taking all of my art classes at the Cambridge Center for Adult Education. I enrolled in three evening art classes, and they were hard. They were "real" classes, in the sense that we had live models we would draw and then all of the students and instructors critiqued the work: basically everything I needed to learn that wasn't offered at Harvard. The art classes were essential to my getting into Yale. If I had stuck with the art classes at Harvard, I simply wouldn't have gotten into the theatre program at Yale. I remember Ming Cho Lee telling me that I had to know how to draw.

While I was going to school at Harvard, Robert Brustein was just starting the American Repertory Theater at that time, and he brought all of these people up from Yale to Cambridge to start this theatre company, and Michael Yeargan was one of them. I remember that I sought him out and sort of latched onto him from the start and said, "I want to be a set designer, what do I need to do?" He let me assist him on some projects that he was doing with Robert at the time, but he recommended that I go on to graduate school and try to get into Yale, where he was also on the faculty. Although I had to take courses in costumes, lighting, and all that, I always knew that I wanted to design sets.

I then went to Yale to get my Master of Fine Arts, which was great in terms of design training. We actually had very little discussion or training in, as you put it, "the business of show business"; in terms of how you conduct your life, how you make a living once you're done with school. People have asked me why I don't teach, and I really struggle with my answer, which is basically, "Well, it's really hard to make a living as a professional designer, so why would I teach it?" I feel incredibly fortunate that I barely scratch out a living as a set designer. Given that I live in New York City and I work as hard as anybody in this profession, it is still hard to make a go of it.

Q: With that said, why do you do it, then?

A: I do this work because I love it, and I feel like I was made to do it. Honestly, though, if I couldn't design as much as I do, I probably would have gone and done something else. I basically stumbled into this during college, fell in love with it, and immediately thought, *OK, this is what I have to do.*

Q: What is it about designing sets that excites you?

A: I would say the primary reason I do this work is because I get the chance to be creative. My favorite part of the whole process is coming up with ideas for each individual show. I think this is related to storytelling in that you can come up with an idea, but if you can't tell the story, then the idea isn't of much use. I also really enjoy being a team member, but I can't say that it's my favorite part of the job. I guess it depends on the team with whom you are working. Again, it's coming up with the idea, and seeing that idea come to fruition, that's the most exciting part for me.

I would also say that I'm more about the emotional part of theatre and conveying the story. I do like the technology and craft

Top: Production photo, Derek McLane Studio
Anything Goes, Stephen Sondheim Theatre, New York, NY, 2011
Directed by Kathleen Marshall
Lighting, Peter Kaczorowski
Costume, Martin Pakledinaz
Set, Derek McLane
Bottom: Set model, Derek McLane

of theatre—especially the craft, because it is so important to design a set properly in order to help tell the story. Technology is definitely important, but if you don't know your craft and the set is badly drafted, designed, built, or executed, then the idea falls apart. These things are enormously important to me, and I'm pretty relentless about them.

Q: Do you think that there's something about your personality that led you to theatre, as opposed to something more permanent, like architecture or some other profession that could offer more stability?

A: Actually, I did think about other professions. I had a favorite uncle who was an architect and he was a big influence on me when I was a teenager. Part of me thought that I didn't want to become an architect because my uncle was such a huge force of nature, and I wasn't like that. Also, I'm very impatient and I think theatre designers in general are impatient people. The turnaround on theatre projects is relatively quick and I like that. I get to see my designs come to fruition relatively quickly, and I'm always interested in what worked and didn't work. To me, that's exciting.

Q: Do you make regular shop visits to check on the build for your design?

A: I used to, but not as much anymore; there just isn't time. Also, most of the shops aren't near New York City like they used to be. For example, if you want to visit the shop that is handling your design, you have to drive two to three hours to get there. Once you're there, you'll want to spend at least two hours looking over the set, and that alone takes up most of the day. For that alone, I delegate those tasks to my assistants. I'm very fortunate to have two assistants whom I trust. All of us have the same tastes and seem to be

"Technology is definitely important, but if you don't know your craft and the set is badly drafted, designed, built, or executed, then the idea falls apart."

in sync with one another artistically. Also, they send me a lot of pictures. This has become a really easy way to communicate. They can literally snap a picture with their phone, send it to me, and I can tell them what I think.

Q: How many assistant or associate designers do you tend to have working with you?

A: I usually hire around five assistants before the Tony season, because everyone wants their show up right before the deadline. I'll drop back to my usual number of two assistants when Tony season is over. There's just no way two assistants can handle all of the work when the Tonys are coming up.

Q: How do you delegate the work amongst them? Are both of your main assistants trained to handle everything?

A: Yes and no. My assistants are well trained to do just about anything I ask of them, but they each have their own skills and strengths, so I try to give them the things that they are especially good at. Some of it also has to do with their individual personalities and working with directors and shops. For instance, if I know that a certain director is tricky to work with, I assess which assistant has the personality to best deal with the director. Or, if one of my assistants already knows the director of a particular show, I will pair them up because they do already know each other.

Q: Can you talk a little bit about the pros and cons of being a New York-based designer?

A: I used to only work in regional theatres. One of the things that eventually became frustrating for me was I felt like the shows didn't necessarily always meet my expectations. It seemed like there was always some kind of compromising going on when it came to the casting, and that rarely, if ever, seems true in New York. There is such an enormous pool of talent to choose from that there isn't compromising in this city. I also eventually got frustrated with doing all of these shows that my friends and colleagues never saw. Doing a show in Milwaukee or St. Louis might be great, but I don't really have friends or family in either of those places, so I felt like my work was invisible in many ways. I really wanted to work in "my backyard"; I wanted to work where people that I knew could see it and we could have a conversation about it and I would feel that my work was more a part of my life. Being able to work in the city is a very big "pro." My family is here. My friends are here. I really like that.

Q: Are there any negatives to working in New York City?

A: Oh yes. In the New York theatre scene, your work is judged more harshly. If something doesn't go well, an entire production can get shut down pretty quickly. New York can be very harsh in that way. The scheduling also tends to be a bit insane because everything is constantly in flux, whereas in regional theatre they may schedule something a year in advance and they really stick to those dates. That kind of scheduling just doesn't happen in New York City. Even the nonprofits—it all just tends to be chaos. It depends on what actors are available; projects can come together and just fall apart. Also, regional theatres tend to have really good craftspeople that are in residence and that you can really rely on. They can do a lot of really amazing design work without killing the budget of the show. That tends not to exist in New York theatre. There are great craftspeople in New York, but they aren't affiliated with any institution, but rather are freelance.

One of the harder things to get used to in New York—which I had a difficult time adjusting to, but am now totally used to—is that there is no theatre company. There's no sort of producing infrastructure, so every show that you take on is completely from scratch. The entire production has to be created from scratch every time. To me, it is just the weirdest thing! Having just done *How to Succeed in Business*, *Anything Goes*, and *Bengal Tiger at the Bagdad Zoo*—all three are big Broadway projects, and we had to basically invent the company that was going to make each one. For each production, we had to choose a production supervisor, props people, and the shop that was going to build it. The costume designer had to choose the craftspeople and the shops that were going to create the clothes. The lighting designer had to deal with the staffing of that department. It's just all of these disparate people that have been brought together to work on this one project. It tends to help if you've worked with these people before, and it also helps if you know the designers or have worked with them or the director. It helps because it can be a bit of a challenge if you're working with all new people who've never worked as a team. I remember my first couple of Broadway shows, I felt really stung by that concept: the whole experience of working with a group of people who were strangers. We all just met in a room one day and said, "Let's put on a show." I think that it's really hard to create a good show that way.

Q: How do you continue to educate yourself on the constantly changing technology in this field?

A. I will confess that I do not know how to draft on a computer. I never really learned how to, and I don't feel as if I need to learn it at this point. I don't really draft by hand at this point, either. I'm quite capable of evaluating and criticizing a sheet of computer drafting—whether it's well drawn, is clear, that sort of thing. We do a lot of hybrid work in our studio where we draw things by hand and then import it to CAD. I'm quite adept at Photoshop. I blocked out some time after one of my children was born about twelve years ago and while the baby slept, I spent most of that time teaching myself Photoshop.

Q: Do you do all of the renderings for your designs, or do you hire others to do them?

A: Well, for the most part, I don't really do renderings. I only do renderings for the corporate projects. Corporate projects always need renderings. With theatre projects, I create a lot of doodles, and I always do them myself. They are very much kind of crude, working drawings, almost like napkin sketches, and I do tons of those. I have to do those myself because that's my thinking process. After that, we tend to build models.

Q: Are they traditional, physical models or digital models?

A: They are always physical models. We also do a lot of rough drafts and models. It's not uncommon for us to do six, seven, or eight really quick studies in the model form. We can do six or seven versions of a model in about a week when it is necessary.

Q: Do you tend to add color after the white model is complete, or are you thinking in terms of color all along the way?

A: It depends on the project. Sometimes I see the color right away, from the very beginning. But that doesn't mean that I will use color in the model. Usually I have a strong image of what I want, and I will describe it. I tend to think of things more in relation to the shape, volume, and space of the project.

Q: You mentioned that it is difficult to make a living as a freelance designer. Can you talk a bit about the sacrifices you have had to make in order to continue with this career?

A: Well, my wife brings in an income, and without it there's no way that we could have afforded to raise three kids in Manhattan on a set designer's income. Quite honestly, the only reason we could afford to raise the kids and also live in Manhattan was because of my wife's contribution. In that regard, I can't honestly say I made a sacrifice

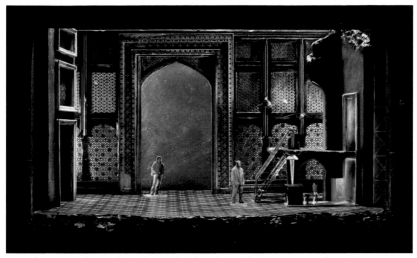

Bengal Tiger at the Bagdad Zoo, Richard Rodgers Theatre, New York, NY, 2011
Directed by Moisés Kaufman
Lighting, David Lander
Costume, David Zinn
Set, Derek McLane
Scenic model

with our living location. I think the sacrifices I make have more to do with the amount of time I spend working as opposed to the time I get to spend playing with my kids. However, I think this is the case for a lot of people, regardless of their profession. For example, there are a lot of evenings that I'm not home because I'm at rehearsal. On the other hand, I've taken advantage of the flexibility of my schedule. I'm able to attend my kids' sporting events and school concerts because I can schedule my work around these important things in my life. I've been out of town on occasion for some of my children's events, but for the most part, I've been around. I'm also able to take longer vacations than some guy who works on Wall Street, for example. I get about five weeks of vacation with my kids every year. I think I've been a very involved father and have a good balance between my work and my family time.

Q: What is your creative approach to a play or musical?

A: I think my approach is pretty organic for each piece. First, I read the play. After that, I talk to the director and we both start talking about how things [in the play] should be. Sometimes the director will have a strong take on the piece, and sometimes I will have a strong take on it. Sometimes neither will feel any certain way about a piece, so we brainstorm to come up with ideas as to what it could be. I really try to let the ideas evolve without immediately imposing anything on the piece. I also always wait to begin researching or sketching until after I've met with the director.

Q: Do you continue to design in the regional theatre circuit, or is your focus here in New York?

A: I really don't design regionally anymore unless I think it's something that will come to New York. Pretty much all of the work I've done with Moisés Kaufman, from *Bengal Tiger at the Bagdad Zoo* to *33 Variations* to *I Am My Own Wife,* all started in regional theatre. Sometimes these plays were done in a couple of regional theatres before they made it to Broadway.

I don't particularly like going out of town because I really enjoy being in New York and being near my wife and family. Sometimes going out of town is just part of the process. I made a conscious effort to give that up when my first child was born, which was eighteen years ago. We were living here in New York and at that point in my career I decided that I really wanted to start working in New York and not just doing regional theatre away from home. I had actually turned down a lot of little off-off-Broadway shows because the money was so bad and I thought, *I can't afford to do this.* And it was actually my wife who suggested that I stop turning those opportunities down. She said the problem was that nobody in New York knew who I was because I was only doing regional theatre work. It didn't mean anything to the New York theatre world that I had a great regional theatre career because they only see what they see. So if I wanted work in New York, I needed to start working in New York. It was kind of rough because there I was, thirty-five years old, and I was starting to do these little shows again for no money. I sort of forced myself to do it because I needed to get myself into the New York theatre scene. It was by doing those small, no- or low-budget shows that I began to really develop relationships with the people I'm working with today. It was a bit strange because I was no longer assisting and I was still doing regional theatre work while I was taking these little New York shows.

Q. At one point this season you had four shows that opened in the course of ten days. When you have that many shows going on at the same time, do you ever feel that your creative bank is empty?

A: No, I never have felt depleted in that way. There are times when I read something and I don't know what I want to do with it right away—

that definitely happens. I don't think it's due to being depleted, but rather that I haven't discovered the right ideas yet. Sometimes, I can, but other times, if the clock is ticking much too fast and I have yet to discover the right ideas, I will just start drawing. I just draw as much as I can and trust that I will eventually come up with my right idea. It's painful, because when you start drawing without an idea, the sketches are terrible. You end up creating one terrible sketch after another. Even though you've now drawn all of these terrible sketches, usually something useful does come out of it, because it leads you to figure out how you're going to fix what is wrong with the idea. You begin to ask yourself what it would take to make it a good idea and move forward with it.

Q: How important is it to do proper research before you begin to sketch?

A: I do a lot of research. A lot of times I look at photography books. For example, looking at the real moon to get a sense of how it should look in a design; I use photography books a lot in those cases. Then there are the specific books that are more useful for capturing the feel of a certain period, or finding the correct type of architecture that should be used. So there are a number of different directions I go with my research.

Q. I'd like you to talk about collaborating with the rest of your design members. How often do all of you, as members of a production team, sit around a table and actually discuss the production?

A: Not very often. Usually, there are one or two meetings like that for each show. The thing about set design is it usually has to start much earlier than the costuming, for example. It's just a purely logistical thing: the simple fact that building scenery is going to take longer than anything else, and there's a lot of money riding on it, so it has to get started sooner.

Another aspect of being the set designer is that the set is also going to define so many stylistic and spatial things that it would almost be impossible to start the lighting design before the set design, because the set is going to define the style, architecture, and mood of the production. I think you could certainly start the costumes at the same time as starting the set design. But, I think a lot of times the director wants to start that process with the set designer at the beginning, so they can discover what the world of the show is—and there are times when the director doesn't know. They may have an image in their head of what they want, but in order to make their image more tangible they rely on the set designer to help them. I think some directors definitely like working that way; collaborating with the set designer from the beginning and then introducing other design team members.

Q: When you work with the same design team and director often, as you do with lighting designer David Lander and director Moisés Kaufman, does the "shorthand" that you develop help in the creative process?

A: Oh, absolutely it helps. You have a shared vocabulary where you are able to say things like, "Well, we don't want it to be like that!" Or sometimes you can be somewhat shameless and say, "What I was thinking you would do here is similar to what you did on such-and-such we did together." So it definitely helps.

Q: How important is it to you to take vacations and downtime away from the business of theatre?

A: I try to incorporate a little downtime on a somewhat regular basis. Like this morning, I actually slept in late. I was extremely tired and needed to catch up on sleep from the week before, when I was in tech every night. For the most part, I enjoy going to museums and art galleries. Sometimes if I need to catch up on my reading, I will do that at home and not come into the studio. I also love going to Europe when I can. I usually try to connect that trip with some kind of work that I'm doing and then try to spend a little time just being there.

Q: Do you have a schedule that you try to stick to that involves working out or going to the gym?

A: I do go to the gym; probably not as often as I should. For instance, I rode my bike to work today. When it works out schedule- and weather-wise, I try to ride my bike every day. I also try to go running. On my last show, I was really stuck in tech the entire time, so I would slip out for a few minutes and go run the stairs about twenty times just to do something. For the most part, I think I'm pretty fit and healthy. As I've gotten older, I've become more careful about what I eat and avoid the temptation of eating at night while I'm in tech, which is what I always used to do.

Q: Do you read all of the critics' and bloggers' work pertaining to shows you design?

A: No, I don't read any of the blogs, and I don't read all of the critics, either. I sort of glance at what they write, I guess, but I do specifically avoid bloggers because I find that they enjoy being unduly negative. I

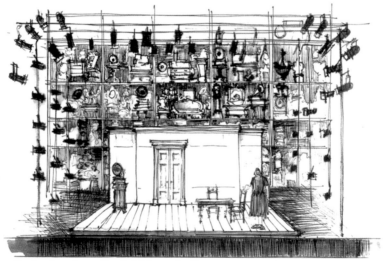

Top: Production photo, Derek McLane Studio
I Am My Own Wife, Lyceum Theatre, New York, NY, 2003
Directed by Moisés Kaufman
Lighting, David Lander
Costume, Janice Pytel
Set, Derek McLane
Bottom: Set sketch, Derek McLane

feel like with a newspaper critic they are at least accountable to their editor. Bloggers aren't accountable in that way. I'm just too sensitive to read something that was written to intentionally hurt.

Q: When you graduated from Yale, did your class of graduates stick together?

A: No. We all scattered to the wind, except for Kathy Zuber and me. Kathy and I went to Yale, and we've been best friends ever since. Going to Yale was not a factor in my getting professional work. It may have encouraged people to hire me, like knowing certain people from Yale who coincidentally knew someone in the theatre and then recommended me for hire. It was that sort of thing that got me work, not the fact that I went to Yale.

Q: Do you remember your first New York design? What it was? Where it was? How you got it?

A: I actually do remember my first project. It was a show at La MaMa E.T.C. but I can't remember how I got it. I remember that it was a play about Kafka, but I'd have to look it up to be absolutely sure about that even. Ellen Stewart was running La MaMa at that time and she taught me the rules. One of those rules was that I had to build the set. She also made it clear that there couldn't be any green in the set—and if there was any green in the set, I would have to repaint it. I remember she said, "La Mama don't allow no green." She said that I would be paid $300, and, if the show did OK, she would try to pay me a little extra. Every day she would come into the theatre and say, "Oh, sweetheart, what do you need?" And I'd say, "Well, I really need a carpet." And she'd say, "What kind of carpet?" And I said, "An oriental carpet." And she'd say, "OK, let's go up to my apartment." So, we'd climb up the five flights of stairs to her apartment, which was above La MaMa, and she'd say, "You want that carpet?" And I said, "Yeah that would be great." "OK, roll it up and take it downstairs." So, I just kept taking stuff from her apartment until I finally had the whole set furnished.

I got my $300 fee, and Ellen and I became good friends. One day she said, "Come here sweetheart, I want to give you a hug." She gave me a long hug, and as she finished hugging me she kind of felt my butt a little bit; at least that's what I thought at that moment. Well, a little later when I went to get on the subway, I reached in my back pocket to get my wallet, and as I pulled my hand out of my pocket, a little piece of paper fell to the ground. I picked up the piece of paper and it was a crumpled up check from Ellen for $250. So instead of grabbing my butt like I thought, she had actually stuffed this check into my back pants pocket.

Q: Did you do a lot of assisting when you first came to New York, and if so, was that how you built your relationships?

A: Yes, that's part of how it happened. I assisted a lot to survive, financially. Going back to one of your earlier questions about how I learned the business, that's how and when I learned about this business—by assisting other designers. I also learned by watching those designers and seeing what they did, overhearing their phone conversations and learning how they dealt with situations and directors and producers. I learned a huge amount about this business just by listening. One thing I can't stress enough is for young people to have patience. It takes a really long time to develop relationships that will eventually pay off in the end. It just takes a really long time. I've been in this business for over twenty-five years now; it's such a slow process of meeting people and developing trust with them.

Q: Regarding the Union: Were you forced to join after designing so much regional work, or did you join right out of grad school?

A: I actually joined the Union while I was in graduate school. I joined during my second year. It was because Ming Cho Lee insisted that we all take the exam while we were in our second year of graduate school, so everyone that graduated was already a member of the Union—everyone in my graduating class, anyway.

Q: How do you deal with your design contracts?

A: Now, my agent looks at them. There are projects that we will pass on because the money is so poor and it's just unacceptable. He will also give me advice when I ask. If it's a good deal, he will advise me to take it, or if he thinks it's not such a great deal, he will say, "I think we can do

"One thing I can't stress enough is for young people to have patience. It takes a really long time to develop relationships that will eventually pay off in the end."

better than this." The advantage of having an agent like that is he sees a lot of deals, not just mine, so he has a much more objective sense of what's out there and what is a good deal and what is not a good deal. Also, having an agent takes away the nastiness of negotiating, because inevitably, nastiness can occur, and I have to work with those people.

Q: When you came to New York after attending Yale, did you have set goals that you wanted to accomplish or did you have the mindset of just wanting to work?

A: No. I've never been that organized. I think it's great if some people think they can do that—set goals and meet them by a certain time or age—and are that organized. I've certainly set goals for myself, but they've been much more general. For example, I used to never design musicals, I just wanted to do plays, but then I decided I wanted to design a musical. So, I set that as a goal for myself; I really set out to land a musical design. I told everyone I came across that I was interested in doing a musical and I took some designs for small musicals as a way to get an opportunity for a bigger one.

Q: Do you think people tend to get pigeonholed in this industry?

A: Yeah, I actually do. I certainly do my best to avoid it. I really want to show diversity in my projects.

Q: Do you work certain hours in your studio, or is it basically working from whenever to whenever?

A: I work somewhat regular hours that fall between 9:30 AM and about 6:00 PM, but it tends to vary depending on the workload. My associates work much more regular hours than I do.

Q: Do you share the studio with other designers?

A: Yes. It's nice on a lot of levels. For one, it's cost-effective. It's also more likely that someone will be here to receive a package as opposed to if I worked here alone. There's also a wonderful little sense of community, which is nice.

Q: How important was it to acquire a studio that was away from home?

A: It was very important to my career. Getting my own studio was a big step forward. When I first started working, I worked out of my apartment, so getting a studio was definitely a big, big deal, in that I was professionalizing what I did.

Q: When you have production meetings at your studio, are producers involved?

A: Usually if it's a producer's meeting, they want to have it in their office. But there are a lot of other meetings where the producers do not attend, like the meetings we have where we discuss scene changes, transitions, that sort of thing. The assistants, like the assistant directors and assistant stage managers, attend them here, mainly because it's a relatively convenient place to meet. And we don't want to necessarily have those meetings in the producer's office simply because we want to be able to talk freely about everything.

Q: With regard to Tony season, it seems like you can go months and months without being really busy, and then suddenly you are buried in design work. With so much going on, how do you maintain that creative focus?

A: This past spring was a little more challenging than usual because so many shows were opening simultaneously. But I had really good associates on each of those projects, so I always had a person assigned to one show who could serve as a representative for me. Having the same person assigned to each show allowed for continuity. If there was a problem, one of my associates would text me, and I'd literally jump on my bike and zip right over to the theatre. I could literally go from theatre to theatre through Times Square in about four minutes.

Q: How far in advance do you try to keep yourself scheduled?

A: I'm pretty heavily scheduled in the fall, and right now everything is pretty much up in the air for spring 2012. I have several possible shows, but nothing is on paper yet. Besides, a lot of scheduling for spring won't happen until June 2011. A lot of projects seem to come together in June. Once Tony season is over, everyone begins to shift his or her focus to the new season.

Q: On a show—like *How to Succeed in Business Without Really Trying*—that has had many revivals, what kind of pressures do you feel, designing a show that has already undergone many different designs because of the multiple revivals of that particular show?

A: Well, you obviously want to design something that is your own, definitely. You'd like to think that your design is an improvement on every design that has been done before, if that's possible! Also, you don't want to repeat what's been done, so it is a delicate thing.

Sometimes I won't even look at any of the previous designs, just so I can go into the project with a clean slate. Even though I've lived in New York for over twenty-five years, I had never seen a production of *How to Succeed in Business Without Really Trying.*

Q: How early on in those shows do you become involved in the rehearsal process?

A: I usually try to go on the first day of rehearsal so I can meet everybody. Then I usually stay away for a while. It really depends on the show. With musicals, I'm more involved with the rehearsal because there is so much choreography involved, and I need to be there to make sure the actors can interact well with the space. Again, it really just depends on each show. Unless a director calls and tells me he needs me right away because something isn't working, I generally stay out of the rehearsal space for the first two weeks, and then become the most involved toward the end of rehearsals.

Q: So, the collaborating happens in the rehearsal hall?

A: Yes. That certainly happened on *One Arm* at the Acorn Theatre, and it certainly happened on *Marie and Bruce*, written by Wallace Shawn, which we did with the New Group here in New York. I had designed this one particular piece of furniture that basically became everything, which was quite tricky. I needed to have prototypes of the furniture built so the actors could familiarize themselves with them. That led to phone calls from Scott Elliott, the director, where he was concerned about some aspects of the scenic pieces. I would then go over to the rehearsal to work with them and make the necessary changes so the actor was comfortable using them. That's also another interesting part of my job; when a director needs something that hadn't been accounted for in the original budget, in this case a prototype of some scenic element, it is my job to go back to the producers to ask for more money to build what they need. Surprisingly, it usually all works out.

Q: What would tell a young person who really wants to be a designer and is coming from somewhere outside of New York City?

A: Well first of all, it's really hard to get work here. I would suggest that you try to find a way to connect with a person that you are interested in working with. Write an email, send a letter, and just try to make contact with people who are currently working in theatre. I don't think that a résumé is really going to impress anyone in New

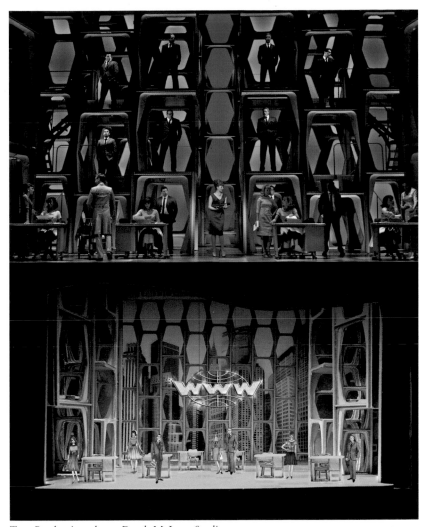

Top: Production photo, Derek McLane Studio
How to Succeed in Business Without Really Trying, Al Hirschfeld Theatre, New York, NY, 2011
Directed by Rob Ashford
Lighting, Howell Binkley
Costume, Catherine Zuber
Set, Derek McLane
Bottom: Scenic model, Derek McLane

York City. If someone sends me a résumé, I just look at the school they attended, and that's about it. Listing the shows that you've worked on in college unfortunately really doesn't mean that much. I would rather see a really compelling piece of drafting.

If I were to draft a letter of introduction to get somebody's attention, I'd write a note that specifically talked about that person's work, what I knew about their work, and why it appealed to me. I'd make it really specific to that person, and include a really dynamite image of either some piece of design work or drafting that I had created. I'm personally more interested in how people can draft. I'm looking for a really good draftsperson. It's a really good skill to have. A lot of people are just mediocre, and a really good draftsperson is hard to find. I also want someone who can draw. Honestly, something well-drafted is more important to me than a beautifully crafted set design. All they would need to do is attach one kickass, knock-'em-dead design, along with a very specific note, and that is really all I would need to evaluate them.

Unfortunately, that's not what I get. I receive hundreds of emails with too much information on their résumé and a generic message about how they would like to work in my firm. I don't even have a firm! They usually don't know anything about me. If you are going to take the time to write to someone, make sure you do your homework on that person before sending a letter.

Q: Do you think a designer who is just getting started should take any and all design projects regardless of the fee?

A: Well, it really depends on the project. Even though the project may be in New York, it still may not be worth doing. Not everything that is done in this city is going to be beneficial to your career, but that's also the really difficult thing to distinguish; figuring out and deciding if you should do it is the hard part.

Q: Do you have any final advice you'd like to give to a young designer?

A: It is really tricky. Really, I don't think I even know a good answer to this question, because as a young designer you basically need to come in and start working doing whatever you can just to make a living. Plus the design jobs you will get are so impossibly small with such tiny budgets, that it's just damn near impossible to be able to create anything that even looks like anything, if that makes sense! So, I think that it's a real catch-22 for young designers in that situation. They want to do the design job and be a part of a production and be seen;

however, they can't actually do a full design. So it begs the question, does doing certain design jobs, unfinished-looking designs, actually help these young designers? The answer, I think, usually is if they can manage to have an idea and be clear with that idea, it might help them to establish a relationship with the director who isn't too frustrated by the lack of resources. Then that relationship is what I think ultimately matters, because if the director goes on to something bigger, he may take that designer with him. To this day, even though I work quite a bit on Broadway, a lot of my design choices have to do with the director I'm working with. I want to work with certain directors because we have a great working relationship, and if that means working at a small off-Broadway theatre as opposed to a Broadway house, so be it.

SCOTT PASK – SET DESIGNER
Wednesday, February 9, 2011

Designer Scott Pask generously took time to chat with me at his apartment in Manhattan before he had to dash off to another technical rehearsal for The Book of Mormon, *a Broadway musical from the creators of the hit television show* South Park *and the recent Broadway hit,* Avenue Q. *He was also in the final stages of preparing to open the Broadway revival of John Guare's* The House of Blue Leaves, *with a cast that featured Edie Falco, Jennifer Jason Leigh, and Ben Stiller.*

His professional career has taken him from the Broadway stages, where he has had a number of hits including The Book of Mormon, *the revivals of* Hair, Promises, Promises, Nine, Take Me Out, *and* A Steady Rain, *which starred Daniel Craig and Hugh Jackman, all the way to England, where he has designed sets and costumes for the National Theatre, the Almeida Theatre, the Donmar Warehouse, and numerous West End productions.*

Not only is Scott Pask one of the hardest working designers in New York City, he's also one of the most acclaimed working in this business today. His designs have garnered him numerous awards, which include a Tony win for his work on The Pillowman, *another Tony that he shared with co-set designer, Bob Crowley, for* The Coast of Utopia Parts I, II, & III, *and his most recent Tony for the design of* The Book of Mormon.

Q: Did you attend a lot of theatre while you were growing up?

A: I saw *The King and I* with Yul Brynner in San Diego when I was young and was always fascinated with the Tony Awards broadcast on television. Even though I hadn't seen a lot of it growing up, I was definitely intrigued by it. The drama building in Tucson was across the street from the Fine Arts Complex. I had taken one set design course there, which had fueled that interest.

Q: Where did you receive your training and with whom did you study design?

A: I grew up in Yuma, Arizona and did my undergraduate work at the University of Arizona College of Architecture because I loved drawing when I was young. I was particularly fond of drawing houses, and I would jump in the car with my dad and go and look at them when we were traveling anywhere. I knew that the program in Tucson was great, and having been awarded a scholarship to attend made my decision that much easier. Tucson was also a place I loved; going to school there was really great for me. I think that working and learning within a program that was heavily weighted towards architectural responses to the environment and region, as opposed to, say, prioritizing the emotional or processional content of a space, encouraged my design search beyond the traditional field of architecture. For me, those poetic considerations were the most exciting. I loved my education there and consider the University of Arizona the place where I formed myself as well as my ideas about space. Later, I did my graduate design studies at the Yale School of Drama.

I've gone back to Tucson to visit and speak with students there a number of times and stay in close touch with the head of the program in Production Design and Technology. I'm still drawn to Tucson—my taste in architecture is a response to the austerity and ruggedness of that environment, as is my craving for and harmony with a horizon line. And it provides the background against which I look at other places. Even when I was a student there, I was looking beyond that home base. A professor who was very influential suggested I study abroad. So I went to Florence, Italy through Syracuse University and found that being in such a different environment was hugely eye-opening for me.

Q: If you were an architecture student, what motivated you to walk over to the theatre department?

A: I was fascinated by the idea of finding alternatives to concerns of function and the physical environment as the inspiration point for my design. I had the beginnings of ideas about narrative and emotions as the springboard for making artistic choices. So I began talking to Chuck O'Connor, who was the head of the set design program. I brought one of my architecture models over and talked to him about the program and my interests. Technically, I couldn't take the set design course; it was reserved for majors and required a number of prerequisites that I didn't have. But he could see I was very serious about it, so he got me the approval to take the course. I absolutely loved it. I did a design project for *Measure for Measure*, which, ironically, I happen to be designing right now for the Delacorte Theatre in Central Park this summer. Chuck was an amazing teacher.

Q: How long were you in Italy and how did it play a role in your future career choices?

A: I was there just one spring semester. Then, the following summer, I traveled to Greece with friends and ended up working for an architect in Santorini. It was right before that trip to Greece that I began to realize I was interested in a more narrative approach to making space, as opposed to the traditional practice of architecture.

I did see a little bit of opera while in Florence, but really my time there was about the architecture. In Florence, the architecture students were separated from the rest of the Syracuse program in our own apartments and studios, and we traveled every weekend. We did not take the intensive language courses or live with host families because of our travel obligations. In our sketchbook course, we visually analyzed and drew everything from the architectural details to the civic planning of the cities we visited. It was an amazing way to see all of Italy. Seeing that much, so intensely, was incredible—a fantastic experience. And I was this kid who didn't even have a proper winter coat. I had this London Fog with a liner, and I thought I was doing great! I was from the Arizona desert; I was a little green to say the least.

What I remember being so important to me then, and I still believe it to be important today, was the experience of seeing. The Baroque and High Renaissance architects were really shaping space with intense emotional content. Striving to evoke that emotional reaction was huge, really huge in my development as a designer. I remember specifically recognizing the Italian Baroque duality between Bernini, the darling of Rome and the popes with his beautiful, swirling columns and Borromini, the darker, more rebellious architect.

Oh, and the colonnade out in front of Saint Peter's. At the heart of experiencing Saint Peter's is the incredible curved colonnade approach. As you walk down, you don't see the terminus, and you're in this state of anticipation—building and building anticipation, and you can't see around, until you finally get to the point of presentation

"What I remember being so important to me then, and I still believe it to be important today, was the experience of seeing."

when the cathedral is at its most impressive. That's what I took away from seeing and experiencing Saint Peter's: the whole idea of the emotion in perceiving space and the sense of procession being really important. That was not something I had encountered in my architecture training before coming to Italy.

Q: After the semester in Italy you said you remained there for the following summer. Was that for pleasure or for work?

A: After I finished school in Italy, I went to Greece for sightseeing and didn't want to leave Santorini because it was so beautiful, so I found a job with an architect there. It was great to be immersed in regional architecture. The designs I worked on were remodels and additions to private homes. If someone wanted to extend their house, they just dug deeper into the side of a cliff. It was so rustic and incredible, and, in many ways, not unrelated to the regional approach in the desert where I grew up.

     While I was there, I also saw a lot of funerary architecture and began to understand how people in Europe were really in touch with that aspect of the cycle of life. I had also been to the Carlo Scarpa-designed Brion-Vega Cemetery in Italy. All of these beautiful spaces shaped around interment and for the comfort of mourners and visitors were really influential. When I came back to Arizona, my architecture thesis was a funerary complex set in the desert outside of the town where I grew up. It was about procession and about trying to encapsulate the modern idea of using raw materials in a sensitive way. The project ended up looking like a ruin set on the side of a mesa and was pretty dramatic. I look back now on that summer of 1989 as being such a wonderful year for me and my discovery of what I was going to do with my life.

Q: So I assume travel abroad is something you highly recommend to all young designers.

A: Most certainly. You can study about all of these places from books and in classrooms, but until you are actually in the spaces, you don't fully understand them. I remember one chapel, Borromini's San Carlo alle QuattroFontane; I wrote a paper about it when I returned home. I remember going into this little chapel and when I got inside, the perspective was so distorted. It was an amazing, fluid space, and the walls appeared to slip and melt into the punctured pattern of the ceiling, making the very shallow dome look as if it extended for miles. The chapel was a huge influence on me, and the theatricality of that wonderful space was so memorable.

Q: How long after you graduated from Arizona did you wait to go to graduate school?

A: After I graduated from Arizona, I came to New York and worked for five years. That, to me, was really important. It was important that I came and worked and really found my footing and made a living in whatever I could do. It was while I was in Greece that I made the decision to go to New York and eventually study with Ming Cho Lee at Yale. It was my set design professor, Chuck O'Connor, who told me, "If you want to pursue this, you should think about a graduate program." The book *American Set Design* also helped.

Q: What was your experience like at Yale?

A: It was great. I have immense respect for Ming. I think he is one of America's great modernists. I feel that in the same way I love Louis Kahn and other great modernists of American architecture. I have a similar appreciation for Ming and his contribution as a great contemporary theatre designer. He is incredibly generous with his time and is passionate about what he does, so I have great memories of studying with him and with the other brilliant teachers who were also creating their own important work at the same time. What was so wonderful about those three years was getting the reinforcement that helped me stay on the right path. I attended graduate school to further my skills and understanding of design for theatre, and the intensity of the program there was exactly what I wanted.

Q: Did you ever feel that because you didn't have a degree in drama before attending Yale you were at a disadvantage?

A: On the contrary, I was often so happy that I got a degree in architecture before coming to graduate school for theatre. I really think that by bringing another perspective into the theatre world, it helped me to grow as a designer. It was the architecture and art history, and even spending time in the sculpture department at Yale, that allowed me to bring new approaches and ideas to my work.

Q: Were you drawn to theatre for the collaborative nature of the art form?

A: At the time that I started exploring theatre, I was very much immersed in my own design work and studies and really just searching for the medium that would inspire me the most. Today, my design work is a balance between quiet alone time, researching and sketching ideas, and developing approaches with the director and my colleagues on the creative team. That kind of collaboration is a very fulfilling aspect of the process for me.

Q: What was your first break once you graduated from Yale?

A: The very first thing was a job I got following the portfolio review (Ming Cho Lee's infamous Clambake) to design the premiere of Kia Corthron's play *Splash Hatch on the E Going Down* at New York Stage and Film's main stage.

Q: In addition to design work in New York City, did you seek out other employment in order to support yourself?

A: My first job was working for the fashion designer Paul Smith at his store on Fifth Avenue. I did help out on some window displays and once did the Christmas windows, but I was more on the shop floor as a salesperson. I had such a great time working there—it was really fun. I mean, I was twenty or twenty-one, in New York, making a living, and at the time I was living in an apartment with a couple of other friends, one of whom was from the Italy program. I definitely learned things while I was working for Paul Smith; I learned about tailoring, which is helpful when I do costumes now. More than anything, it was great to just find my footing in the city and be able to make ends meet to stay here.

After work, I would often work with this artist I'd met through friends, Huck Snyder. He was a part of the downtown East Village art scene that was going on during the 1980s. At the time I met him, he was working with the performance artist John Kelly, and I assisted them on a number of projects. I also remember actually being in one piece, *Maybe It's Cold Outside,* at the Kitchen on West Nineteenth Street back in 1990. I worked with John and Huck for a couple of years on John's pieces. I basically stumbled into the performance art/dance world. A number of the younger dancers would have their pieces performed at Dance Theatre Workshop, and they would ask me to design for them. So it was really through all of these dancers and through my work with Huck and John that I started designing for dance.

Q: Was it during your time working with Huck Snyder and John Kelly that you developed your interest in film work?

A: It was actually in 1992, while I was working at Paul Smith, that I interned part-time on a movie that Stuart Wurtzel was designing called *Romeo Is Bleeding*; I interned in the art department on my days off. The art director was incredibly supportive of my work. During that time, I happened to be at a party where I met an independent film production designer. After hearing about what I was doing, she asked if I would be interested in meeting further about art-directing a film with her. I agreed, and we did the film, *Postcards from America*, and together we did a number of other projects as well.

I do love film. I art-directed *Living in Oblivion* and then did another film the summer before I went to Yale, which allowed me to save some money for school. The summer between my first and second years of graduate school, I worked on a kids' television show and another film in the art departments. It was really helpful to be able to offset some of my school expenses. The people I worked for were very kind and allowed me to fit the work into the three months I had between the spring and fall terms.

Q: When you are working on multiple shows at once, can it get confusing keeping them all separate?

A: Actually, no. Sometimes little things from one project cross-pollinate and inform another one in an interesting and unexpected way. I might see something while I'm working on a particular show and I will say, "Oh, that's what I need for another show," whether it's inspiration or a lampshade. I just did a shop visit for *The Book of Mormon,* and while I was there, I saw this patch of ice on the ground outside. I thought to myself, *That is the floor for* The House of Blue Leaves. I took a picture of it, and it ultimately became the reference for the surface treatment for the floor surrounding the apartment.

Everything seems to continually feed the creative nature of the work for me. I like keeping things fluid. I feel like if I only have one project going, it could become overwrought. I pay intense attention to each of them, and because I get to do what I love, it doesn't feel like work. It's not my job, it's my passion, and it makes me happy to have a number of ideas percolating.

Q: Did you find it difficult, financially, to live in New York?

A: When I first got out of school, I had a little apartment in the East Village. Having an inexpensive apartment afforded me the freedom to do a lot of theatre projects. By not having huge living expenses, I was allowed a lot more breadth of decision-making about work. I guess the point of me sharing this is if you can be judicious about your personal living arrangements, you're not forced into the stress of having to bring in a ton of money just to keep a roof over your head. You will be able to take work that doesn't necessarily pay a lot, but still keeps you visible and fulfilled as an artist.

Q: When did you finally realize that the workload you were taking on as a designer was just too great and you needed help? When did you finally hire an assistant?

A: I think it was pretty early on, while I still had my studio in my East Village apartment. I began work on a large project for a musical, which would ultimately tour, and I needed additional hands to help with drafting and in the model. That need continued as I began to do a number of off-Broadway and larger scale shows.

Q: Do you remember your first job on Broadway and how you got it?

A: I was hired to be the associate scenic designer on *Cabaret* for its move to Studio 54. I was drawn to the project because I respected the designer, Robert Brill, a lot and the main thrust of the project was to turn Studio 54 into the Kit Kat Club. It was going to be an architectural experience, and I was really excited to devote great attention to those details. After that, Robert and I designed a project together at the Roundabout that was directed by Joe Mantello called the *Mineola Twins*. [Scott and Robert won both the Lucille Lortel and the Henry Hewes awards for scenic design for this production in 1999.]

Q: What was your first design that made it to Broadway?

A: It was *Urinetown: The Musical.* I began work on *Urinetown* when it was being developed off-Broadway after the New York International Fringe Festival. I was brought in to work with the director John Rando [who ultimately won the Tony for his direction of *Urinetown* when it moved to Broadway the next season]. Off-Broadway, it was in a space just down the street from Studio 54 called the American Theatre of Actors. It was interesting because ultimately the set became an architectural installation. It was in a theatre with no traditional stage house equipment. I removed the existing black proscenium frame and designed a catwalk surrounding the room and the audience, reinventing the experience of that space.

After it opened, it became a hit and soon moved to Broadway. The design was deeply integrated into its environment, and it had to be re-imagined for a traditional proscenium theatre. Luckily, the interior of Henry Miller's Theatre [now named the Stephen Sondheim Theatre] was in pretty rough shape. I was able to begin the design with the audience's experience out on the street by boarding up the front of the theatre with plywood. The whole interior was painted black and aged, the balcony boxes were cinder-blocked shut, and I designed a new catwalk system that reached beyond the proscenium into the house and up to the balcony seating level to create a really immersive experience. People would remark on how amazing it was to see the back wall of the theatre and its beautiful windows exposed, never realizing that it was a completely scenic wall with a crossover and prop storage behind it. The design looked as if the windows were boarded up and filled with fluorescent light fixtures and the band was in an industrial mesh storage cage stage right. [Brian MacDevitt, a frequent collaborator, was the lighting designer.] It was a thrilling show to be involved with, and to have it be my Broadway debut was fantastic.

Q: Did you join USA-829 immediately after graduating from Yale?

A: No, I didn't really need to join right away. I joined in advance of my work on *Cabaret* at Studio 54. At that point, I was able to join through a portfolio review and courses for working designers rather than the traditional exam.

Q: When you came to New York, did you set specific goals for yourself as a designer?

A: Not really. I didn't really know the path, but I knew I had to keep moving forward and designing. *Splash Hatch* was great for me since it happened immediately after graduation and allowed me to continue on the creative momentum from school. Then in the fall, I designed an opera and then a John Kelly project. Luckily, a kind of continuum began to develop.

Q: How large is your current design support team?

A: It is usually between four and five. Right now, I have Frank Mc-Cullough working with me on *The Book of Mormon*, Christine Peters on *The Book of Mormon* and *The House of Blue Leaves*, Orit Jacoby Carroll on the Shakespeare plays for the Public Theatre in Central Park, and Lauren Alvarez, who is working on the models for all of those projects. Frank has worked with me frequently since *The Coast of Utopia*, and Orit has been working with me for more than ten years and is an incredibly important part of this very collaborative process.

Q: Do you find collaboration to be something that is fairly consistent or is it dependant on the individual production?

A: I find that it is very director dependent and does vary with each individual production. At times, the entire creative team is very much engaged in the early stages of development; other times, that interaction happens later in rehearsal and in the theatre. One of the largest

Pal Joey, Studio 54, New York, NY, 2008
Directed by Joe Mantello
Lighting, Paul Gallo
Costume, William Ivey Long
Set, Scott Pask
Scenic model, Scott Pask Studio

creative teams I've worked with was on *The Coast of Utopia*, Parts I, II, and III. With two scenic designers and three lighting designers, in addition to the costume, sound, and projection designers, it could have been a challenge of competing priorities and personalities; instead, guided by director Jack O'Brien's inspired vision, everyone's input enriched the overall experience and the work reflected that integrated creativity. This spring, *Live Design Magazine* selected it as one of Broadway's top ten designs of the last forty years.

Another important facet of collaboration in theatre is between the designer and the technical teams of a production physically creating the built work. You rely on teams of engineers, craftspeople, and artists to understand and interpret your work and to bring their own skills to the mix to ideally make the work even better. You learn to make your ideas very clear and to be a decision maker.

Q: Do you have an example illustrating that point?

A: Right now, we are working on *The House of Blue Leaves*, and I have this sky piece that is like nothing I've ever done or seen before. I had this meeting with the director, David Cromer, and we had a sort of "arts and crafts" day in my studio, experimenting with clay and paper. We ended up honing in on an idea that was more sculptural than a traditional sky drop. We agreed that the play called for something more complex and that this would help inform the audience that this was an unsettling place.

Once I developed this idea into a sculptural paper model piece, I worked with the scenic artists to try and come up with samples for the process. They were looking at the model, and seeing exactly what it should look like, but weren't sure how to fabricate it in reality. I said to them, "The one thing that is important is the idea of gravity. I don't want to have a sense of gravity when I look at it. The fabric has to appear to defy the laws of gravity." The scenic artists ended up developing a complex process of "sculpting" the fabric, so it ended up having the wonderful sense of buoyancy created in the model. Being able to articulate the idea in terms of gravity and buoyancy allowed the scenic artists to draw on their wealth of techniques to create exactly what I was looking to achieve.

Q: Collaboration also requires a very special ability to communicate effectively, don't you agree?

A: Absolutely. Communication is about finding the right words to share and not just talking. You really have to communicate the intent. So much of our collaboration and communication is about clarity—being clear with your ideas and then finding the right vocabulary to communicate those ideas. It's possible to be sitting with the finished model and have it be totally clear, but there will still be five ways to accomplish it. It could be done using papier-mâché, or it could be carved foam, or it could be making it out of real found objects and piling them up; there are so many factors that go into the decision-making process. Your job as the designer is to direct and refine that process in order to arrive at your visual and conceptual goals.

"Communication is about finding the right words to share and not just talking."

Production photo, Scott Pask Studio
The House of Blue Leaves, Walter Kerr Theatre, New York, NY, 2011
Directed by David Cromer
Lighting, Brian MacDevitt
Costume, Jane Greenwood
Set, Scott Pask

Q: Were there any surprises you encountered in this industry?

A: One thing I didn't really know when I was first entering drama school was the sheer number of hours you spend in the theatre! But the biggest surprise was probably the extent to which the process takes place in a public forum. The work is quite personal, and at the same time open to such wide scrutiny.

Q: What do you turn to for inspiration if your creative "tank" is getting low?

A: Well, I am a member of the Metropolitan Museum and the Museum of Modern Art, and I visit them both quite a lot. I will always go through the collections, and the littlest things I see can manifest themselves in unexpected ways. It may seem completely unrelated at the time, but somehow becomes inspirational later on. I also change my physical environment, especially going back to the desert in Arizona.

Q: How do you take care of yourself in this hectic business and in a city like New York, where the winters can be brutal?

A: Climate and my immediate surroundings absolutely factor into it. I overheard someone on the subway saying, "You know, this winter has been soul-crushing." I find that I just have to take better care of myself, especially during the tech process. I do like to go to the gym regularly. You want to be feeling your best to do your best work. I know when I am eating well and exercising, I am more focused, and I just feel better.

Q: What other projects outside of traditional theatre are you currently working on?

A: I am doing the Orchid Show this year at the Botanical Garden here in New York City, which is a whole other amazing world. I hope it's also a step toward achieving my fantasy of designing a float in the Rose Bowl Parade! My personal artistic tastes are so austere that the idea of a floral extravaganza is such a rich contrast. Taking a single orchid, which is so beautiful and sculptural alone, and then creating something completely different with a mass of orchids in all different colors and varieties has been wonderful. The theatricality and drama of it is exciting.

   The curator of the project contacted a friend and colleague of mine, Drew Hodges, who is also responsible for a lot of theatrical advertising here in New York and is an inspiring person to me. When we're involved in the same theatre projects, I find that I want to spend time with him, and he wants to see what I'm working on in order to inform his process of developing a visual identity for the advertising. The idea of making a theatrically themed design for the Orchid Show and collaborating with him was very intriguing.

   What I suggested was to approach the project from a dramatic point of view rather than replicate theatre iconography. The idea of procession was really important in this design. I thought the idea of compressing viewers through a colonnade in the exhibition hall and then exploding them out into one of the larger Palm Courts was exciting. I wanted to explore how we could use each orchid in multitudes to create a theatrical environment and evoke a dramatic experience for the visitor. It was really fun to say, "Here is the 'diva' orchid, and they're the scene stealers. These are the 'chorus' orchids, impressive in great numbers." We also created a quintessential Broadway proscenium out of orchids that turned out to be really stunning, even crafting curtains from swagged burgundy garden hoses. I'm also working on a Cirque du Soleil show for 2012 and the 2011 Council of Fashion

Designers of America Fashion Awards show set, which I've done for a number of years.

Q: Do you tend to keep yourself booked solid as far in advance as you can, or do you like to leave some "wiggle" room for other projects that may come up?

A: It depends. I currently have plans to work on a show in 2013, and the Cirque project I've been working on for a while opens in 2012, but I try to leave room for a project that might pop up that would be amazing to work on. Too many things have happened during my professional work experiences that have forced project dates to change, that I try my best to have some schedule flexibility, though sometimes it's difficult. For example, I've had a project suddenly enter the picture when an actor became unexpectedly available. And if you are completely booked solid, it just eradicates the possibility of those instantaneous projects. That sort of thing happens very quickly and there's really no way to plan for it either.

A couple of summers ago, a great theatre project came up very last minute due to an actor's unavailability, and the director called to see if I was available. At the time I was contemplating a movie project that I was slated to design. Since I hadn't done a film in a while, I was excited about this project, which I thought had really interesting visual potential. The film was still very early in the process. Both were in New York City, so it was completely feasible that they could work out one after the other, but as it turned out, the film never got green lit, and I ended up doing two theatre pieces instead. I think it takes a special skill set to be able to balance a career in film along with theatre projects.

The thing about keeping holes in your schedule is that things just appear out of the ether. The phone will ring and you never know who is on the other end of the line. If you book yourself solid, you may miss those wonderfully magical surprises in the world of possibility.

Q: You must really enjoy the lifestyle of freelance work in order to live with the uncertainty of not knowing what or where your next project may be.

A: It is certainly something I have become accustomed to since it's inherently a part of this business. I love when I have something in six months to look forward to and something in a year to look forward to. I don't like feeling anxious about not having enough work ahead of me, but leaving room to be open to surprises can be exciting; you just have to have faith that it will be OK. You have to listen to your heart and trust that it's serving your big-picture vision, even if your head is not 100 percent sure what that happens to be. When I decided to walk across the street and into the drama department back in 1987, there was no path taking me there; I just knew I was looking for something that was a combination of architecture, emotional and narrative content, along with sharing a room with a bunch of other people. When I figured out that it was the theatre, it was absolutely instinctual. I can't tell you how lucky I feel to be doing what I love.

Q: It sounds like you made a serious decision after graduate school to really focus on theatre work instead of film or dance. Was that the case?

A: I really did, especially since I had just spent three years studying it. Right after I graduated from Yale, I was considering a production design position on a wonderful film, but I also remember thinking that I really wanted to do theatre. I always feel like my path has treated me well. You do, however, always have that sense of the "sliding door" question: If I had chosen door "A," what would I be doing, or if I had chosen door "B," would I be doing something completely different? You never really know where your path is headed, but I couldn't be happier for how mine has turned out so far.

Q: How do you prefer to begin the actual design process? Do you use the computer, or do you draw by hand?

A: I always sketch by hand. I am constantly drawing. Early in the process, I will fuss around with the initial models before turning them over to my assistants for finished model work. For *The House of Blue Leaves* I was making copies and scanning and printing out and cutting up and gluing back together just to see where it took me. For the Shakespeare projects that I'm working on at the Delacorte Theater in Central Park, I was drawing more than modeling. That particular show moved from the sketch to the model to the drafting and then to construction very quickly.

"You have to listen to your heart and trust that it's serving your big-picture vision, even if your head is not 100 percent sure what that happens to be."

Q: What about visual research? How does that play into your work?

A: I am a research hound. I love research! Each show I design has a binder, sometimes multiple binders (especially for the musicals), filled with reference materials, each one meticulously organized, and I refer to these throughout the design process. The studio also keeps very clear archives. When I'm working on a show, I might recall a detail I came across previously but didn't use at the time that would be perfect for inspiring something in a new design.

Q: Since you prefer to draw by hand, are you a fan of the digital drawing software that is available?

A: I do think that the hand-to-eye connection is the quickest way for me to communicate my ideas. There is no shortage of instances where I was sitting at a meeting discussing an idea with a director and, as we're talking, I will begin to scribble out an idea on a piece of paper, then show it and say, "What do you think of this idea?" Recently, I was sitting right here with John Doyle and we were figuring out this new musical we're going to be doing together. I literally sat here and as we talked, I sketched out ideas and I was able to clearly show what I had in my mind and get his immediate reaction. I don't feel like I can disengage from the conversation by saying to the director, "Just give me fifteen minutes to work this up on the computer." I want to feel engaged and feel like I am clarifying ideas for us. I need the drawing to become part of the dialogue. Working on the computer, in that way, is not a dialogue for me.

For me, the technology has to be there to expand the process at the appropriate point, but it will never take the place of beginning with conceptual hand sketching for me. There is a spiritual connection between what is in your head and heart and what comes through your hand onto the paper.

Q: Do you enjoy working on revivals of plays and musicals as well as new works?

A: Certainly. With each of the revivals I've done, I have not seen the previous production. I think that has been to my benefit. Since they're new to me, I can approach the pieces fresh. Helping define what is relevant about doing a particular piece today as opposed to twenty years ago is a rewarding challenge.

Q: Do you feel like you have an identifiable "style" in your designs?

A: I try to be a chameleon in my work, in the sense that I respond to the varied context of each show. The results can seem quite different

Top: Scenic sketch
Les Liaisons Dangereuses, American Airlines Theatre, New York, NY, 2008
Directed by Rufus Norris
Lighting, Donald Holder
Costume, Katrina Lindsay
Set, Scott Pask
Bottom: Production photo, Joan Marcus

stylistically on the surface, but there's a consistent "style" or approach to my process. That's why research is so important to me. My designs might reflect period detailing or they might be a conscious reaction against it, but it's always rooted in the specific reality established by the writer's words and the director's interpretation. For example, in *The Pillowman*, the set was dark and ominous and pulled details from 1930s Eastern Bloc architecture and graphic design, but used scrim effects and Grand Guignol theatre techniques to let both the characters and the audience escape through the oppressive walls into the worlds of Katurian's macabre imagination.

Rather than compression and release, *Cry-Baby* was about the collision of convention and rebellion. The shapes of the moving portals first established the staid world of the "Squares," then tilted dramatically to reflect the rebellious nature of the "Drapes" and their reaction to conventional society. Also, the scenery itself reflected the pop colors and textures of the 1950s. These are two very different projects, but both are rooted in a conceptual understanding of the material and the desire to physically portray and support that onstage.

Q: Can you talk a bit about this new project, *The Book of Mormon*, for which you are currently in tech?

A: I hope a lot of new people, those that don't usually go to the theatre, come to see a show like *The Book of Mormon*. People who enjoy *South Park* now have a chance to experience this Broadway musical written by Trey Parker, Matt Stone, and *Avenue Q*'s Bobby Lopez. It's always great to reach an audience that may not normally be accustomed to coming to live theatre, and even a younger audience as well. The show is fantastic—so funny and irreverent, and along with that, it has enormous heart. It shows so hugely the writers' love of the traditional musical theatre form, and the story and songs are amazing.

The Book of Mormon has elements of traditional musical theatre design, viewed within this liturgical frame as the proscenium, so it becomes a kind of "pageant." It's based in the wing and drop tradition, largely because it is in a quite small playhouse, and in this case, is the form best suited for ease in delivering scenery out on the stage and for lighting. It is particularly suited to the show here, as its roots, its story and songs, are very much influenced by the traditions of the great composers, lyricists, and shows of Broadway's golden age.

However, there is a definite break from traditional content, just like the show. The wings, which depict a kind of scorched land-

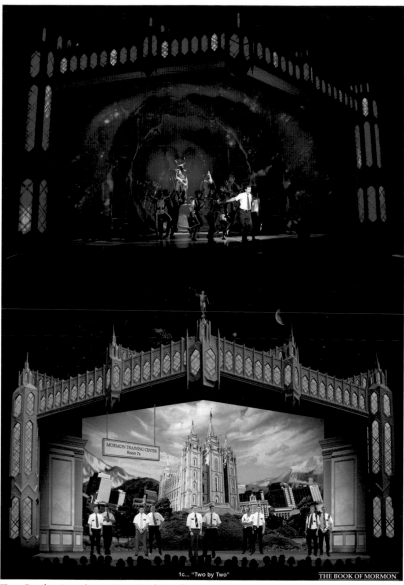

Top: Production photo, Scott Pask Studio
The Book of Mormon, Eugene O'Neill Theatre, New York, NY, 2011
Directed by Trey Parker and Casey Nicholaw
Lighting, Brian MacDevitt
Costume, Ann Roth
Set, Scott Pask
Bottom: Digital rendering, Scott Pask Studio

scape once we arrive in Africa, are tatty, burned, torn, and completely distressed, all within the religious white gleaming portal, with its stained glass. It ultimately looks kind of beautiful. It is a huge contrast to where the musical begins in Utah with bright, shiny, cool colors, each element almost having its own halo, and everything moving magically. The design also has many scenic transitions that happen in front of the audience. Behind the scenes, the crew moves at breakneck pace to create instantaneous shifts from one place to another. Some are actually quite startling, and the entire stage is transformed incredibly fast.

The design process began with research that I would bring to Casey, Trey, Matt, and Bobby, showing them the images I was drawn to. Because the village where the Ugandans live—and where we spend much of the musical—is so important, it was critical to me that the look of it reflects the people in a very real way. The villagers are defending their homes against very real and serious problems. That's where a big part of the show's soul resides, and there's an obligation to be accurate about it, to get it right, and to have that look fit within the artistic context of the vision for the show.

Q: Do you find that others who are in this industry serve as inspiration to you and your work?

A: Absolutely! There are directors and collaborators who I consistently find to be inspiring—in their imaginations and the excellence of their work. Additionally, there are those who also feel like family to me. When we are in the room together on a project, I'm just so happy. We are supportive of each other, and also incredibly involved in the work together, which hopefully makes the look and content of the show ever better and more cohesive, conceptually and physically. And we have a great time!

Q: What three books would you tell every young designer they must have on their shelf?

A: I think you can't do anything without a familiarity with Spiro Kostof's *History of Architecture*. In order to do anything architectural well, I think you have to know proportion and scale and the historical sources of it. That is a great book to cover the bases. When you understand the basics of architecture, you start to understand space. Second would be *Janson's History of Art*. I know these two books seem like basic primer books, but they're necessary; all designers need to have a foundation and understanding of our art and architectural past. Finally, I would pick a book that really strikes you. When I was in school, I would invest in one book for each project and try to find that one book that would really inspire me. I was always trying to build a reference library that was truly personal.

One last specific book I would suggest right now is *Just Kids* by Patti Smith. It's always fascinating for me to hear about an artist's path in a completely narrative form. In this case, it's a poetic recounting of how she made her way in the city, against challenges, and serendipitously met her creative counterpart. She's a wonderful writer and poet, and it's an amazing story of two artists finding their way together and inspiring each other every step of the way.

Q: What is one quality or trait that you would say is the biggest downfall for young people to keep in check?

A: I think it is important to be ambitious about design and passionate about your work, not ambitious for ambition's sake. There are words like "networking" that make me bristle a bit. I have received letters and emails from students and young designers who have written, "I'm coming to New York, and I would love to begin *networking* with you." Maybe it's me, but it just sounds like it comes from the wrong place; it doesn't come from the heart. A better approach would be to know something about the designer with whom you'd like to meet or intern, and be passionate about your work. This way, I can see your excitement and a generosity of spirit; it's those qualities that are so important. I think it's great to be ambitious, but be sure what you're presenting is you and your work, in your most genuine form. Be passionate about it, and make *that* why you are ambitious.

There's a costume designer whose work I thought was so fantastic when I saw it at a graduate school portfolio review, and although I had never met her, I wrote her an email and said, "I can't believe your renderings! They are so incredible." She was so touched that I contacted her that I asked her to come to the studio and work with us. She came and did an illustration for a musical I was working on that was beautiful. I then asked her to do a couple of other things, and it was because I wanted to help her in whatever way I could, and, in a way, her spirit was inspiring to me. Her drawings were otherworldly. They were so beautiful and I told her, "In addition to costume design, you should really think about illustration." Her renderings were so inspiring, and although the final costumes were beautiful as well, I felt she needed to share her gift of the renderings with others, too. If not, those beautiful drawings would be lost to all but a few people.

Q: What about portfolio pieces? What should a young person coming to New York have in his or her portfolio?

A: At school, we always did classic plays and operas for design projects, and I understand why, especially since I am looking at so many young people's portfolios. Those classics are really important to a portfolio, because otherwise I am seeing their work but I don't remotely know what the play is about. It's great that people are working on new plays, and I understand completely that often on these projects the design vision has to be refined due to the environment or budget or what have you. And I think it is great to have those new works in your portfolio. But all I can really say is, "Wow, that looks great. I have no idea what it's about, but I think that looks fascinating." Even with explanation, it's one sided. I will always be excited to see someone have a Shakespeare or an Ibsen or an August Wilson in their portfolio, so we can have a dialogue.

There has to be a balance. There should be a couple of pieces in your portfolio that can lead to a conversation about the play and your choices. It's about having the opportunity to have a common bond so when you walk into those interviews, the conversations can be productive. Those classics are really important to have in your portfolio for sure. It is more about sharing rather than if you have ten projects I don't know at all. When that happens, I begin to feel isolated, and all I can do is respond to what they are telling me, and I can't engage with you and ask questions about the play and your ideas.

In many ways, by seeing those classics in your portfolio, I can also access your tastes and your point of departure for a piece. I can sense modernism and sense if you understand what is contemporary by the way you handle *Measure for Measure,* or *The Tempest,* or even *Buried Child* or whatever classic piece it happens to be. What are you doing with these plays to make them yours and contemporary?

It reminds me of when I did *Buried Child* early in that undergrad scenic design class. I presented the sketches for my initial design approach, and all it was was a giant baby crib. And the teacher said, "That's very interesting. But now take that idea and translate it into what this exercise was about, which was to then do a realistic set. Take your information and think about how you would make it appear to be child-like in a realistic environment." And he was completely right that the concept had to be translated. So what I did was create slightly over-scaled furniture and had wallpaper on the walls that was in pastels and flaking off. It was great for me, because what I had initially created was essentially a dance piece and I was told, "OK, now apply that same feeling to an environment where we can really do the play." So just by bumping up the scale of the room and the furniture just a little bit, so the people appeared just a bit smaller, but not so much that it was comical, pushed it just to the level where it was unsettling. There is a fine line between sophistication of scale that is noticeable and something that becomes conspicuous, where it is perceived as intentional but not over the top. Having an honest conversation with my mentor on that project proved to be incredibly helpful in my understanding of how a design goes through a transformation in order to be truly successful.

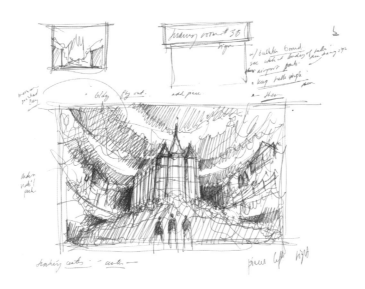

Top: Preliminary sketch, Scott Pask
The Book of Mormon, Eugene O'Neill Theatre, New York, NY, 2011
Directed by Trey Parker and Casey Nicholaw
Set, Scott Pask
Lights, Brian MacDevitt
Costumes, Ann Roth

Bottom: Production photo, Scott Pask Studio

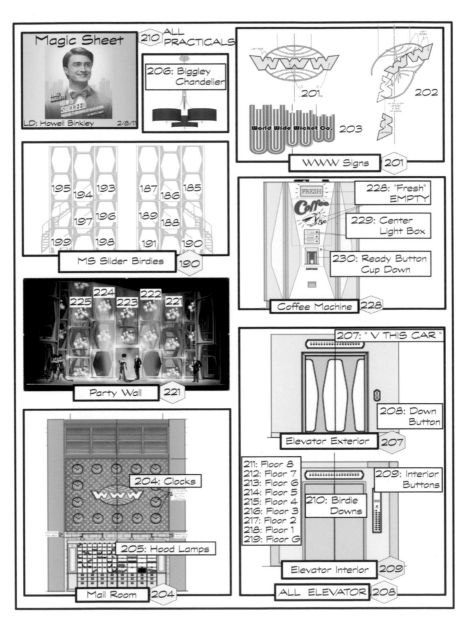

Magic sheet, Howell Binkley Studio
How to Succeed in Business Without Really Trying, Al Hirschfeld Theatre, New York, NY, 2011

Set sketch, Scott Pask
A Steady Rain, Gerald Schoenfeld Theatre, New York, NY, 2009

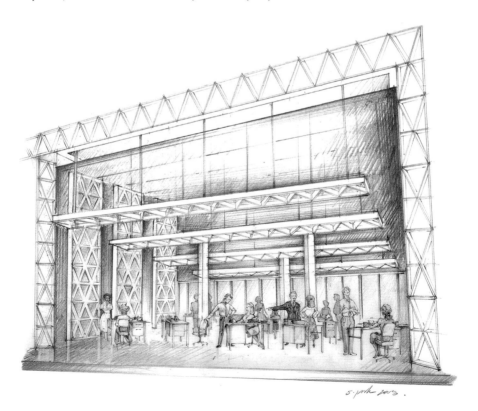

Set sketch, Scott Pask
9 to 5: The Musical, Marquis Theatre, New York, NY, 2009

Regency Room—WHITE CHRISTMAS

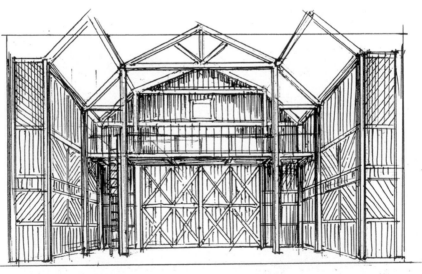

WHITE CHRISTMAS   Barn

Thumbnail sketches, Anna Louizos
White Christmas, Marquis Theatre, New York, NY, 2009

Production Photo, Howell Binkley Studio
Xanadu, Helen Hayes Theatre, New York, NY, 2007
Directed by Christopher Ashley
Set, David Gallo
Lights, Howell Binkley
Costumes, David Zinn

Production photo, Howell Binkley Studio
Xanadu, Helen Hayes Theatre, New York, NY, 2007
Directed by Christopher Ashley
Set, David Gallo
Lights, Howell Binkley
Costumes, David Zinn

Painter's elevation, Scott Pask Studio
Hair, Al Hirschfeld Theatre, New York, NY, 2009

Production photo, Scott Pask Studio
Pillowman, Booth Theatre, New York, NY, 2005
Directed by John Crowley
Sets, Scott Pask
Lights, Brian MacDevitt
Costumes, Scott Pask

WHITE CHRISTMAS   ED SULLIVAN SHOW

WHITE CHRISTMAS   ED SULLIVAN SHOW.

Thumbnail sketches, Anna Louizos
White Christmas, Marquis Theatre, New York, NY, 2009

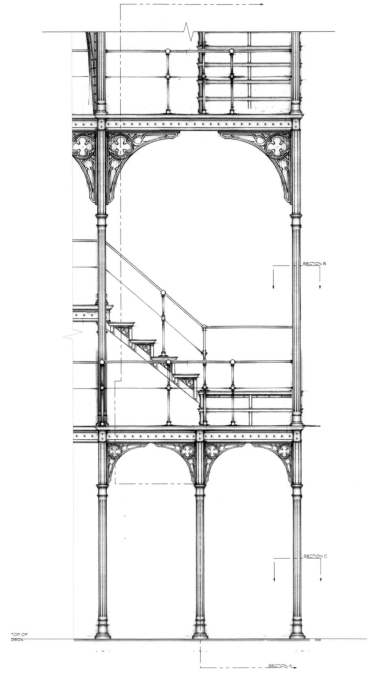

SECTION B

SECTION C

SECTION A

TOP OF
DECK

FRONT ELEVATION DETAIL
3A Scale: 1" = 1'-0"

Design front elevation, Derek McLane Studio
Ragtime, Neil Simon Theatre, New York, NY, 2009

Part II:
Lighting and Projection Designers

KEVIN ADAMS – LIGHTING DESIGNER
Thursday, May 19, 2011

Kevin Adams has been described as a leader in the post-incandescent Broadway era when it comes to stage lighting, primarily due to his exploration of the use of LED technology, neon tubing, and florescent fixtures. He is also known for his bold approach when it comes to color use, which he juxtaposes with intense white light. Given his recent successes—winning the Tony award in 2007 for Spring Awakening, *in 2008 for* The 39 Steps, *and again in 2010 for* American Idiot—*one might get the impression that Kevin is "new" to Broadway, when in fact he has made New York City his home since 1996. Whether he is creating a more traditional design for productions like Chekov's* The Three Sisters *or an explosion of color and movement for something like Diane Paulus and Randy Weiner's* The Donkey Show, *Kevin's work has a look that is uniquely his own. He has truly worked all over this city, from New World Stages to the St. James Theatre.*

Q: How did you get interested in theatre design?

A: I grew up in Texas and had a high school drama teacher who gently persuaded me to look into designing scenery for plays, and I took to it very quickly. I also designed lighting for a few small shows in high school as well. After high school, I went to the University of Texas to study set design and had every intention of becoming a set designer. I ended up getting my Bachelor of Fine Arts and also studied all of the other areas of theatre to include directing and acting. In 1984, I went to Cal Arts to get my Master of Fine Arts in set design. I chose Cal Arts because they had a film design program where they taught art direction and other courses that related to film and at that point in my life, I really thought I wanted to eventually move to Los Angeles to work in music videos, which in 1984 were relatively new. So for two years I studied set design, art direction, and production design without ever taking a lighting design course. I actually had no interest in lighting. In fact, I never really even noticed lighting. In 1986, when I completed my MFA, I moved into Hollywood and worked as a production designer and art director, but ultimately I really wanted to work in live performance; that's really what I found very exciting and I knew it was what I really wanted to do.

Since many of my friends from Cal Arts were artists, I was in the habit of going to gallery openings and museums with them. That was when I started to take notice of how light was being used in various artists' works. Museums in and around Los Angeles had a large collection of space and light work from the 1960s and 1970s in their permanent collections and they often came out of storage and rotated through various exhibitions. Work by Dan Flavin, Robert Irwin, and James Turrell were ones I distinctly remember seeing. I also saw work by new artists like Bruce Nauman and Christian Boltanski. As I saw how they were utilizing lighting as a sculptural form and as a way to frame space in their installations, I began experimenting using similar light-related strategies in lighting my own little sets, and from there it just took off.

This would have been around 1988 to '89. Up until that time, my little set design career was just hobbling along, and immediately when I started lighting my set designs, really interesting local directors and performance artists started calling me to say, "You know that thing you're doing with light? That's how I see my work! Will you come and light my work?" I had to be very up front with them and say, "I will, but please understand that I don't completely know what I'm doing." They would say to me, "That's OK. Let's just try it." I found many of these artists to be very generous and understanding. Somehow I managed to handle it. It was either sink or swim, so I just started swimming.

Working with the performance artists was really interesting because typically it was just the performance artist and I without any other designers, or even a director. Sometimes there was a musician on stage, but it would typically be me, out in the house, responding to the work on stage. I did a lot of that type of work, mostly with Rachel Rosenthal. Eventually I began designing lighting for people who, to this day, I continue to work with here in New York, and who at that time were also living in Los Angeles.

Oddly enough, there was a little weekly publication in Los Angeles, which I think was called *Drama-Logue*. It had job offers in the classified section, and I just remember that they were such sad little jobs that hardly paid anything, mostly actors' showcases. I did find this literary society in Venice that produced theatre called "Beyond Baroque," and I ended up working with them a number of times. They were the people that first let me light my own sets.

So, in a way, it was a small, back-of-the-paper job that ended up turning into my path for a career as a lighting designer. It was really through all of these tiny little projects that I learned how to get a show up. I established great relationships with other designers and directors, and it was those jobs that led to larger projects and also helped me discover more about my voice as a theatre designer. All of those early jobs in L.A. were great experiences. I actually think that to get a large job right away would be far too complicated for a young designer who is just getting started. It's so much better to start small and work your way up as your skills, confidence, and point of view grow.

Q: How did you support yourself during your time in Los Angeles? Designing for performance artists couldn't have paid the bills for you.

A: No, certainly not. Through all of that I continued working as an art director and production designer and I made quite a bit of money, so I could have time off to continue to work in live theatre, which at that time didn't pay very well at all, although Rachel Rosenthal was very generous with me and I toured with her for several years. Also, during my spare time, I was working as a photographer and a videographer. I actually made a nice body of work that really did quite well for me that I'm very proud of. By the time I left Los Angeles in 1996, I was making a decent living as a fine artist, a film worker, and a theatre artist.

Q: Was your theatre work limited to just the L.A./California area?

A: No. I was working a bit regionally and had a few shows in New York at the Public Theatre. Around 1993 I received a National Endowment for the Arts/Theatre Communications Group fellowship to study artist-related strategies of lighting as well as traditional theatre lighting, which resulted in my spending much more time in New York.

Q: Is that the moment you decided to move to New York for good?

A: It was a combination of things really. While I was there I saw that New York was a place I could be—and even more, a place I needed to be. Not in the way that my career was necessarily going to be in New York, but more in the way that it just felt right for me to be here as opposed to being in Los Angeles. Each time I went back to Los Angeles, it would feel odder and odder to be there. Half of my friends had died from HIV/AIDS and the other half had moved to New York, so I just thought, "I really have to get out of here." I just couldn't stay in Los Angeles any longer; there were too many ghosts. So, in 1996 I moved to New York City.

Q: So were the people you knew and worked with back in L.A. your contacts when you got here?

A: Yes. Brian Kulick and I moved here around the same time. He's now the Artistic Director at the Classic Stage Company here in New York and I continue to work with him whenever I get the opportunity. My good friend of some twenty-five years, Mark Wendland, moved here a few months after I did and we continue to do shows together. We just did *Next to Normal*. Oskar Eustis runs the Public Theatre and my good friend David Schweitzer returned here as well to continue directing theatre and opera.

Q: Since you do not have any formal training as a lighting designer, how might that make your work unique when compared to those who've had a more structured, formal training?

A: I think about that from time to time, but it's a bit abstract because of all of the unknowns that are involved. I do feel like I've developed my own, quirky style of designing in a sculptural manner; I guess you could say that it's very scenically based. Having said that, about half the work I do is not in that style; it's approached in a more traditional sense in that I use traditional lighting instruments that are hidden . from the audience to illuminate space and the actors. The other half of my work, the work I consider more sculptural, is done using lighting equipment, whether that's theatre equipment or stuff you can find in a light bulb store. So certainly, there aren't too many people that have that specific point of view.

I also think that my use of saturated color is another distinct trait that some often cite when describing my work. Actually, I think that's what initially attracted people to my work. I remember back in the early 1980s I used to go to dance clubs almost every night, and I would just stare at the people on the dance floor bathed in these intense colors, surrounded by darkness. ·

Q: Does your use of lighting equipment as sculptural items demand that you have a closer relationship between yourself and the set designer, since your lighting equipment becomes part of the scenic environment?

A: Yes. Usually the set designers know what I bring to the table when I am hired. They've either seen my work or, in many cases, we've already worked together. If it's a kind of show that's suitable for sculptural light objects, they're smart enough to expect that I'll want to go down that path. I tend to mostly work with the same people from show to show, and I've been very lucky that they're open to my design aesthetic.

Q: Has your style always been rooted in the use of lighting instruments as sculptural objects?

A: Well, *American Idiot* and *Spring Awakening* are a bit more "rock and roll" than many of my previous designs I guess, but what really happened was I was just beginning to explore many of the new technological advances in lighting fixtures that came out about the same time as those two shows were being conceived. It also coincided with my working with directors who were open to me exploring new fixtures within those productions. It was a bit of luck and synchronicity I suppose.

I would say about one-third of my work incorporates what I call a sculptural use of lighting and about two-thirds does not. Before *Spring Awakening*, it wasn't as prevalent in my work. It was more fully explored in those big "pop rock" shows. In the years before that, you may have seen one or two shows with light bulbs exposed, and then there would be six shows without. I've always been known as the guy who used light bulbs in his work. It's certainly not all I do, but it's always been around. It should also be noted that I did a lot of shows that didn't work out and have long been forgotten, but they were thrilling to work on.

Q: How do you find your assistants? Do you go to showcases throughout the city or do they come to you directly?

A: I mostly work with the same people. I'm not one of those designers who will work every day on a show, and I'm certainly not one of those designers who designs for Broadway every day, so I run a fairly small studio. I had been working with a remarkable associate for the past five years and he recently moved on to the Metropolitan Opera. Oftentimes they are friends of the assistants with whom I'm currently working. Usually I will say to my first assistant, "Who's going to be our second assistant?" And they will know someone that they've either gone to school with or have worked with in the past.

Q: Did you ever work as an assistant designer in New York?

A: Well, I had assisted on a significant amount of shows before coming to the city because my career had already begun out in Los Angeles. It really goes all the way back to my time at Cal Arts, when I was the resident set design assistant at the Mark Taper Forum for one year, which was really great. While I was there I assisted designers like John Lee Beatty, Doug Schmidt, and Ralph Funicello, as well as a number of local designers in the Los Angeles area as a draftsperson and model maker. I also worked as an illustrator, scenic artist, carpenter, and props person in film and theatre, so I had a wide range of practical skills related to set design.

I never really assisted as a lighting designer because by the time I figured out that's what was, I was older, and in some ways I had "paid my dues" in scenery, so I've never assisted or even worked

Production photo, Doug Hamilton
American Idiot, St. James Theatre, New York, NY, 2010
Directed by Michael Mayer
Lighting, Kevin Adams
Costumes, Andrea Lauer
Set, Christine Jones

as an electrician. You have to remember, I was in my thirties when I finally figured out lighting was my path, so it just wasn't where or who I was. But believe me, I certainly paid my dues as an assistant set designer!

Q: When did you join United Scenic Artists – 829?

A: I joined the union in Los Angeles before I moved to New York because I had time to deal with it, and it was a bit easier since I had done some regional theatre shows in the Los Angeles area. It was also around that same time that I acquired an agent, so when I moved to New York, I was set with being in the union and I had an agent.

Q: How would someone describe Kevin Adams the person and Kevin Adams the lighting designer?

A: I think I'm very intuitive. I don't tend to need a lot of input from directors as to where to go with the work. Oh, and I tend to get the "rock and roll" thing, too. Even when I was designing a somewhat conservative production of *Hedda Gabler* on Broadway, the producers would still say, "Oh, it's so rock and roll!"

Q: Was there anything that took you by surprise when you moved to New York to begin life as a freelance designer?

A: The biggest thing that no one ever tells you in school about living in New York is that it's really about real estate. It's incredibly expensive to live and work in New York City. It's a bit less complicated for a lighting designer because we can find little nooks to work in; we don't need as much space, but just *having* studio space can be really tricky, especially if you come out of college with student loans. I don't know how you are supposed to live in New York City in the twenty-first century, have a studio, have an apartment, *and* pay off student loans while working in the arts. That's still a mystery to me.

Q: Can you articulate the biggest difference between working as a theatre artist in Los Angeles as opposed to New York City?

A: You know, when I lived in Los Angeles, I was actually kind of embarrassed to work in theatre because there really wasn't much there, and most of it was showcases for actors. When I met people socially in Los Angeles, I would say that I designed commercials and they were like, "Oh, that's awesome!" They understood that and to them, there's value in that kind of work. If I said I worked in theatre, most people would get a puzzled look on their face, as if to say, "What theatre? We have live theatre in Los Angeles?" That changed greatly after I left L.A., but that's what it was like at the time.

On the other hand, when I arrived in New York in 1996 it was absolutely thrilling that you could go to the corner deli and hear people talking about shows. It's great to be a part of that community and not be embarrassed by that affiliation. New York City, like other large cities, is also just a great place to experience new things. Whether it's fashion or architecture or a new gallery exhibit that's opened up, there's so much to absorb here as an artist. I love being surrounded by others who are creating and making while I too am spending my time creating and making.

Q: Have you been able to support yourself solely on your freelance work as a lighting designer for theatre or has there been other work that you've done as well?

A: Yes, the majority of my work has been live theatre, but I've also done some event design that I found interesting. I also worked on an HBO film *Mildred Pierce* for a while, which I enjoyed quite a bit, but mostly I've worked in live performance since moving here.

Q: Does your design approach change for each type of theatre you do or is it pretty standard for all work?

A: It's different for each and every project. Even within the realm of musical theatre, each show is approached and tackled on its own terms. Not only because there are different collaborators involved, but also, the time allowed for the production or the financial support or the size of the event can affect how I approach each project. You're faced with certain problems that need to be solved whether it's in a regional theatre or on a Broadway stage, and it's my job to get the show up in a way that the audience can respond to and be entertained or engaged by it. The same problem-solving techniques are used in both instances. You start at the beginning with a blank slate and hopefully arrive at the end with a fully realized design.

Q: How do you handle input on your work from people who may be outside of the creative team working on a particular project?

A: Often those kinds of comments are filtered through the director, so I generally don't have to deal with them. You do, however, have to be open to every clue that comes your way. Sometimes people will say something that may or may not necessarily be directed toward you and your work, but they will say something in general about the show. Oftentimes there are clues hidden within those comments that you can take from and it will explain things that may have needed explaining. You have to be open to all kinds of direct and indirect signals. If it's a producer whom I know well and can trust, then it's a different story. I'll often go to them and ask them about the work. It's all about the relationships you have and the trust you've built over the years.

Q: How do you approach the research phase of designing lighting?

A: I'm actually always going to galleries and museums and watching American films from the past. I'm also looking at fashion photography and architecture just about every day, so I'm basically in "research" mode on a daily basis either for projects that I'm in the process of working on or for future projects that I may not yet know about.

I also think some plays or operas don't need additional research. It goes back to that idea of being fully developed as a human being. I tend to be able to pull ideas out of my previous visual experience to get through those types of projects. I don't feel like I need to experience the light in a Brooklyn brownstone to properly light a show that is set in a Brooklyn brownstone.

Now, these "pop rock" musical events that I tend to design require an exploration of the contemporary world in a way that other projects probably do not, and that, to me, is most definitely research. Those shows need to look like they are an event from now, and should respond to a wide variety of modern devices such as what's going on in Times Square, in other theatres, and in current technology and communication. It's not the same as doing research into German farm homes in 1892, but there is a type of research into what is going on in the world right now and how I respond to it by making an event that is equally contemporary. When we were working on *Spring Awakening*, we would spend hours looking at YouTube videos, watching kids acting out pop songs in their bedrooms, because that's what *Spring Awakening* was to us and YouTube was very new then.

I don't usually bring research to design meetings to share with the other members of the team; it's just not how I approach the work. Also, there's a great deal of trust when it comes to designing lighting. Directors and designers are usually working on a number of different projects at once, which typically means people don't have a lot of time to talk about things. When I design plays—especially the simpler plays—the directors will usually trust that I know what I am doing and I can lay out a few basic ground rules as to where I'm going with the piece. They will either say, "Great," or often they'll just say,

"Great. Show me when we get into the theatre." It's very seldom that directors will need to see what you mean by an idea or a concept. It's ultimately about a relationship that's based in mutual trust and finding a common language to share.

Operas, on the other hand, need a bit more time to figure out because the scale is often larger and opera companies generally ask that you sit down and figure out systems and technical needs a year or two in advance, so there's more discussion about design for those types of shows. And Broadway musicals just take a lot of predetermining because there are so many beats inside a musical that have to be figured out ahead of time and they all need to be dynamic and have a varying range of looks.

Q: Do you create storyboards for the directors?

A: No. Usually, and this is not to contradict earlier comments I've made, it's a lot of talking when it comes to musicals. For instance, when we did *American Idiot* and *Spring Awakening*, Michael Mayer, Christine Jones, and I sat down and talked through the entire show over and over and over. Those discussions were related to Michael's staging ideas and the scenery that was involved, and the projections that could be used. We rarely talked about individual lighting looks.

I try to listen to the director and add ideas as I feel they are needed. I actually spend very little time talking about the lighting before I'm in the theatre designing the lighting. There are so many different ways that I will interact with a director that it's typically time and personality driven as to how we work through the project. In that way, I try to stay flexible and open to the needs of the director.

It's really important to be able to work in a situation where it's fully collaborative with all of the other team members present. At the same time, it's equally important to be able to work in a vacuum.

"It's really important to be able to work in a situation where it's fully collaborative with all of the other team members present. At the same time, it's equally important to be able to work in a vacuum."

Truthfully, working in a vacuum happens quite often in theatre. It's really important to be able to come up with ideas on your own, go into the theatre, and implement them by yourself and know that it is on the right track.

Q: When *American Idiot* began at Berkley Rep, was the show conceived fully or was it a scaled-back version that was fully realized once it came to Broadway?

A: I sort of did the same thing with *Spring Awakening* and *Passing Strange* as I did with *American Idiot*. I knew (or I should say, hoped) that they would all go on to be done again, so I tried very hard to keep the original productions within what the producing organization could manage. I tried not to make them too large and not box myself in with a lot of ideas that I may not need or be able to realize. I tried to "sketch" in ideas at the original venues in a way that still looked really good, and then I would let the producers know that I could add another layer of detail in on top of that "sketch" idea, which would usually mean the addition of more specific equipment.

When I first talked with the producers of *Spring Awakening*, I thought it would be best if we kept it fairly simple for the off-Broadway production so that we could continue to figure out what the show really is. Then if the show comes to Broadway, that's where—like I did with *American Idiot*—I can layer moving lights and additional equipment to achieve the looks we wanted. In those first productions, I believe it's important not to break the bank and concentrate on figuring out what the show is before we throw more design and money at it. What was kind of unique to both *Spring Awakening* and *American Idiot* was that even after the fairly lengthy tech and preview periods, we went back near the end of both runs to do additional work.

Q: Do you tend to work only in your studio or do you work at home as well?

A: I like to work at home as well as in my studio. I have a little studio that was next door to where I used to live, but I really like to work in my home. I like to have a paper plot laid out on a table and work on it a couple hours a day. I don't like to sit down and do it in one long session. I like to work for a few hours a day on each plot and get it completed in about a week or two. I also have a house in Upstate New York that has a number of studios in it, so sometimes I will just go up there to do a plot because I don't really need to be here to do it, and up there, there are fewer city distractions. I really do like to live in my work.

Production photo, Doug Hamilton
Spring Awakening, Eugene O'Neill Theatre, New York, NY, 2006
Directed by Michael Mayer
Lighting, Kevin Adams
Costumes, Susan Hilferty
Set, Christine Jones

Q: Have you embraced all of the new technology when it comes to computers and drafting a plot?

A: You know, I still work with a pencil and it drives theatres absolutely crazy having to print everything out for me! If it's off-Broadway, I will make a hand-drafted plot on top of the scenic plan and then copy that and turn that in. Usually my assistant will roll their eyes and say,

"Just give it to me and I will draft it on the computer for you." It's so much easier to modify once it's in the computer, and it's certainly easier to read than my hand-drafted plot. For Broadway shows, I will do a rough plot, give it to an assistant, and they will turn it into a computer-generated plot.

Believe it or not, I actually enjoy working in pencil. There's something organic about it, and I like having the big picture laid out in front of me. There have been times where I will be erasing something for the fifth time, and I'll roll my eyes and think, "This is so stupid and archaic!" Or when I'm remounting a show for the second or third time and I have to adjust a plot once again—it's those moments where I wish I'd learned those programs. Although, I feel like if I do learn them, then it's yet another thing I'll have to do and I'll have more busywork. Right now it seems to work out great, because I have assistants who are very good at it and it's just one less thing I have to worry about. Honestly, I really like having a plot taped out on my table so that I can walk by it and gaze at it and move things around—I really like the pencil and eraser, too, I guess.

Q: It sounds like you're very private when it comes to creating your plot.

A: Yeah, that's absolutely true. The idea of having people around while I work on the plot makes my skin crawl! I like a calm, quiet, work environment when it comes to creating, whether it's in my studio or in the theatre. I also like the distractions that surround me when I work in my home, too. Now, that's not to say I don't enjoy working with my assistants, because I absolutely do. I certainly collaborate with my assistants; it's just that we find ways to do that in our own homes, separately. They've all contributed in remarkable ways to the shows that I design, and the work I do couldn't be done without them.

Q: How do you maintain a healthy balance between the hectic pace of theatre and your personal life?

A: This may sound strange, but I try very hard not to work on a theatre project everyday. I try to get big chunks of time where I'm not working in theatre and that leaves me time to work on personal projects. Being in tech every day would drive me insane. I spend a lot of time looking at other things–devouring the visual world around me every single day. My house upstate is a great place to go to get away and garden all summer. I try to take the summer off to focus on my garden or just do something creative for myself.

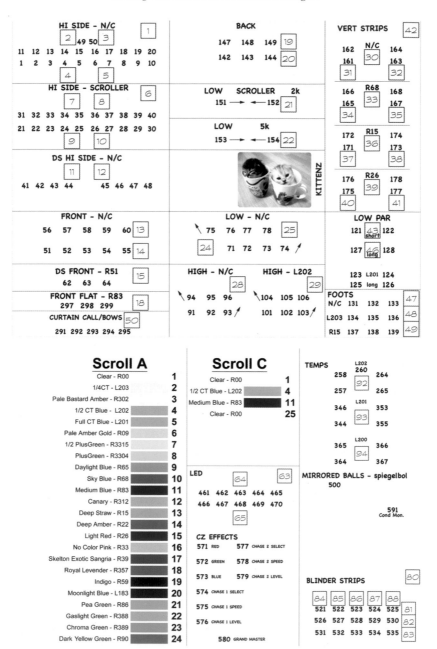

Magic sheet, Kevin Adams
American Idiot, St. James Theatre, New York, NY, 2010

I try to get to the gym on a somewhat regular basis. Unfortunately I am a fairly average, sedentary, New Yorker. When it comes to food, I am terrible at it. I will eat whatever there is. I try to diet, but it's not that easy. I also try to find mental time to escape work, which I think is very important.

Q: You seem to be very selective in the projects you work on and it seems like everything you work on has been a success.

A: Well it seems that way now, but five years ago you wouldn't have said that. The last few years have been remarkable for me, but before that, I did a lot of Broadway shows that came and went. I was working on a lot of shows every year for quite some time and some got noticed and many did not.

Q: Would you council young designers who are just starting off to be selective, or would you tell them they should design everything they can get their hands on?

A: I think you should do things that you want to do, that fit your unique point of view. If there's something that you just don't feel right about doing, I don't think you should do it. If everything that comes around is something you want to do, then you should do all of those things. I just believe you should work on shows and with people you enjoy being around; I've always tried to do that. It's also fine to turn down work that you just don't feel is the right fit for you. I truly believe that being somewhat selective is just fine.

Q: Theatre is such a collaborative art form. Does working closely with others energize you or does it cause you anxiety?

A: As an only child, I enjoy being on my own. Now that I think about it, even when I'm in the theatre, I like to have my "space" where others are not quite as close to me as one might expect. Even though it's collaborative, I'm still trying to figure out all of those relationships in the theatre. It's not that I don't enjoy the relationships I have with my fellow collaborators, because I do. It's just that sometimes I need a bit of peace and quiet to function at my best.

It does seem that the older I get, the more open I'm becoming to really experiencing the people around me with whom I'm working. So, I guess I really do like the social aspects more than I thought; there's just so much anxiety for me that surrounds that social aspect, I sometimes forget how much I really like working with others. It's a very difficult thing to do every day – go into a theatre and not only stay on schedule, but be creative and collaborative and social day in and day out.

Every show starts at "square one" and it's often a long, complicated, new road to figure everything out. There's a great deal of anxiety about having to design in the moment and figure those things out every day. So in many instances, I'm almost always filled with anxiety when I go into the theatre to do my work.

Q: Talk a bit about what you mean by "starting from square one."

A: What I mean is that on every show you have to start from nothing, and there's a long way to go to get to the end of the completed design. It's filled with setbacks and frustrations and full of anxieties. Frankly, it's a lot of work. When you finally get to the end, you realize you've created this complex, complicated "thing" that's made up of a series of smaller, complex "things," and it's absolutely exhausting. Then, when you start a new project, once again, you have to begin the process by figuring out all of the complexities of the show to create a sophisticated, exciting, appropriate design that supports the story being told and the event being presented.

Q: Do you read all of the press on a show you may be working on, such as reviews and things?

A: I read some of that stuff. The reality is, even in this city, no one ever really mentions lighting, and that's a bit frustrating. It seems the less I'm mentioned in reviews, the more awards I win. There was an attitude, back in the 1950s I think, that was developed where people would say, "If it's good lighting, you're not supposed to notice it." I think there are people who still believe that's true, so they decide to not mention it in the reviews.

Q: Do you negotiate your own contracts or do you have a lawyer or agent to do that for you?

A: I have an agent. I also think it's important to understand that in our business, agents don't get you work. They are not agents in the sense that they are out there looking to get you projects. Most of my work either comes through personal and professional contacts or through people who've seen my work. My agent is the person who deals with the negotiations of my contracts, which are very, very complicated, and he's the only person with whom I discuss money. Also, I've just known him for a really long time and he's a good friend who's always there for me when I need advice and he usually knows which work interests me and which work does not.

There are so many different kinds of contracts out there it's mind-boggling. When it comes to designer's fees, that tends to be pretty cut and dry, but it's when you start to talk about the royalties, that's where things get tricky. I still don't fully understand all of that, but he is very good about negotiating those things for me.

Q: Does self-doubt ever creep into your head as you approach a show?

A: Oh, gosh, yes! Almost every time I begin tech it does! Now that I realize that about me, I am able to ignore those feelings. I think that's pretty common though for a lot of artists. The good thing about the theatre is that tech waits for no one; it keeps moving, and you have to go with it or you'll be left behind. There will be moments when I can't figure something out, and then when I get to the next moment, I'm like, "OK, this I understand." Sometimes I'll be with a show that I just can't quite tune in to, but then the next show I'll feel like I understand it so well and I'll begin to feel all of my creative muscles working together. It's during those moments that I'm able to reassure myself that, yes, I do know what I'm doing, and I'm able to do these things quite well. Some shows are just very tricky and you have to struggle through them.

Q: Have you ever been in a situation where you have drawn a blank as to what to do with a certain look or cue?

A: Yes, and I tend to be really honest in those moments. I'll say, "I'm not sure exactly what we need for this moment, so can we move on and come back to that in a little while?" Or I will ask them to tell me a little more about what it is going on in that moment. It often seems to work out where if I don't have an idea for a particular moment, someone else does, and vice versa. It works out that we are all pulling each other along until we all arrive at the end of the journey.

I also try hard not cover it up with a bunch of bullshit. If I don't know what to do I will just say, "Look, I don't know what to do here, and I'm not sure what it's supposed to look like." Oftentimes it will trigger another reaction, indicating perhaps that there is a bigger problem than just this one visual moment. It may oftentimes lead to a discussion about the writing, and we will say, "You know what, something is actually odd about the text here, not the lighting look. I think there is a bigger issue that we need to deal with." It's just good to be honest, because ultimately we are all just human and we have so many things to figure out. I can maybe figure out 80 percent of those things, but I need help with the rest, and I think that's OK to say.

Q: Do you like to work on multiple shows at once or do you tend to focus on one at a time?

A: I try not to do too many shows, but in this business you have to be able to work on multiple shows in one day. Sometimes it may be working on a plot in the morning then going to a lunch meeting with a director then working on another show the rest of the day in the theatre.

A while back I had three shows going up around the same time and as luck would have it, they were all about a block apart from one another. My night would consist of starting at one theatre where I saw the opening of act 1 and from there, I would run over to see the end of an act for show number two, then I would attend a production meeting for the third show later that evening. I was literally power walking between three theatres. Since each show was at a slightly different point in its development, it worked out. If all three had been in tech at the same time, I don't think I could have done it.

Q: Do you attend rehearsals prior to tech week?

A: I do attend rehearsals and enjoy it quite a bit. For some shows I spend quite a bit of time in rehearsals. It all depends on the show. I spend a lot of time at rehearsals when I work with Michael Mayer. I've known him for so many years that I have all kinds of things to say about all different areas when we work together. He's quite open to that and will oftentimes ask my opinion. For example, when we were working on *Spring Awakening* and *American Idiot,* I would spend weeks at rehearsals and workshops just looking and listening—and more than anything just being there for support. I enjoy working with that team of people led by Michael in so many ways.

There are some plays where I will spend a lot less time in rehearsals than others, just because some of the rehearsal rooms are really quite exhausting to be in for any length of time. Between the small size and the horrible florescent lighting, being there for any length of time just saps my energy.

Q: What is the most difficult thing when it comes to being a freelance designer?

A: The one thing you have to understand about freelance designing is that you have to accept that the work will always be up and down. There are very few people in this country who have worked as freelance designers who've had a steady incline in their work. Even if you are Frank Gehry, the work is up and down. There will always be down points in your career where you have to learn not to take it personally. That's incredibly important to your health as a person and as a designer. You have to understand that it's not a comment about you as a person or your ability and talent as a designer; it's just the nature of freelance work.

And in that same vein, you have to have a financial plan in place in order to comfortably live through those ups and downs. I've always been very good at saving money, and throughout my life I've tried to reduce my overhead expenses in order to maximize the profit. It's also important to value money and not blow it on items that are not essential to your life. When I was living in Los Angeles and I was in between film jobs, I would go on unemployment, which I support completely as an artist. It was a great way, financially, to continue to work on my art without starving.

Q: Did you have mentors as you made your way up the ladder as a designer and, if so, how were they helpful to you and your career?

A: Absolutely. Both of my set design teachers at the University of Texas were quite brave to encourage and nurture me the way they did. Of course they taught me great skills, but it is their *encouragement* that I remember to this day.

There were also artists who took me under their wing when I was just starting out. Even now, there are lighting designers who are extremely generous, who've opened their lives up to me with their experiences, knowledge, and encouragement. I think it's important to be in contact with and know those people who are a generation or two older than you, to be able to talk to them about this business and the art of what we do.

Q: When the work gets thin, do you wait for the phone to ring or do you seek out work?

A: I typically wait for the phone to ring. I have to say, I've been extremely lucky, so I might be the wrong person to ask. I think the best advice I can give is to just keep busy. You can learn so much about yourself by collaborating with yourself and having the joy of having no other collaborators. In those situations, the only limitations you face are self-imposed, which is usually determined by the time, energy, and money you can afford to put into those projects. I've always done that, and I still do that to this day.

It's a bit more challenging to respond to the world as an artist when you are collaborating on *The Three Sisters,* but if you're making a video, by yourself, about what's going on in the world around you, you have a much more personal response, and that can be extremely rewarding as an artist. It's a more direct response to what's around you, and I think that's a really healthy thing to do. You learn more about yourself that way. It also feeds your collaborative work—it all connects in some way, if you are able to be open to those connections.

Q: Is there a personality trait or traits that have helped you move forward as a successful designer?

A: Inheriting my mother's optimism has been incredibly useful. I also think being an only child has, in some ways, been beneficial to me. Being optimistic is very important in this business.

Something that's great about being in the theatre is that you're allowed to celebrate who you are, and I'm not just talking about my own experiences of being a gay man. I'm talking about being free to really bring yourself and your voice to the party, so to speak. I've always liked that this kind of work is full of expressive artists, show folk. And to be honest, making a lot of money or being successful in that way was never on my radar growing up in this field. I just wanted to do what I was comfortable doing, which was making theatre for live audiences.

It seems that lots of young people who are coming into the arts, whether it's theatre or fine art, are so business-oriented, so professional, with a goal of needing and wanting to make money and find success. I actually think that between the American graduate school training system and the fact that there's a lot of money to be made in the arts, a great number of young people see this industry differently than I do. They see it as a place to find success and make money, and I'm not convinced that's necessarily a good thing. The thing about trying to do something that is a hit or is successful is great, but what are you going to do on the next show? You can't keep that success and transfer it from one show to the next. If you're just shooting to be successful, you will inevitably fail, because you're bound to the decline of that success.

Q: What books would you recommend that all lighting designers read?

A: I used to read a lot about directors and directing. I think knowing a lot about how directors think and about staging and picture-making is really critical for a lighting designer. Peter Brook's *An Empty Space* is a book I used to read through often. I also think that reading biographies about artists and how they make their work and what their lives are like is really important, too. I also think, as a young lighting designer, watching films on Turner Classic Movies is absolutely enlightening. There's a whole world of remarkable craftspeople who have worked in Hollywood over the last century, and there is a wide array of genres of color and black-and-white movies that can offer a lot to designers.

Q: I know you said that you didn't set goals for your career when you were just starting out in this business, but do you have any goals today?

A: You know, I don't. Recently I was thinking, *How did I get here without ever setting any goals?* But maybe that's actually *how* I got here. All I really want is to keep doing things that are interesting to me and with people I enjoy being around. For me, if I were to set a goal and then not meet it, the disappointment would be awful. I also think if you set goals, you may not look at things that come your way because you have set your eye on a specific goal that may or may not be something that is realistic.

   The problem I have with many goals is that, quite often, they're success related. Success to me just isn't real and, to be honest, I don't know what success means. I think as soon as you buy into trying to achieve success, then you must buy into the lack of success, too, and that can drive people insane. Aging in theatre will naturally drive people insane, and to bind that with being defined by your success—or lack of success—is incredibly dangerous.

Q: What do you like the most about this industry?

A: I love being able to walk to work, and I love being able to wear whatever I want to wear to work! I find that an absolute turn-on about this job. I really love hanging out with show folk, especially actors. I also love talking about whatever I want to talk about with actors. I just enjoy the show business, gypsy world. I like the scheduling of it, which allows me a lot of time off, too. There's a lot to love about what I get to do.

Q: It's obvious that talent and skills are very important, but what other advice would you give to a young designer who is just breaking into this industry?

A: Most young designers don't really have a fully developed sense of themselves and their work and the thing they really need is experience. For about ninety-nine percent of young designers who are just

Production photo, Scott Pask Studio
Hair, Al Hirschfeld Theatre, New York, NY, 2006
Directed by Diane Paulus
Lighting, Kevin Adams
Costumes, Michael McDonald
Set, Scott Pask

out of college, this is the case. Now, certainly there is that one percent who are exceptional and have developed a specific point of view, but for most of us who just get out of school, and I was certainly in that category, the work looks like schoolwork. It just looks like work that hasn't had experience or hasn't yet matured into a unique voice.

I remember when I got out of Cal Arts, I was going around trying to meet the people I thought I was supposed to meet because that's the way you were supposed to do it. But my work, although it was fine, was not completely realized work—it was not the work of a mature artist. It didn't have a point of view. Eventually, I forgot about those people I was supposed to meet and I started becoming interested in making work on my own and working on projects that were interesting to me. Then one day, a few years later, I realized I had made myself into this thing that's a fully developed artist. Suddenly all of those people I wanted to meet started coming to me.

I think my advice would be to focus on developing yourself; develop who you want to be as a designer and an artist, and eventually, but certainly not overnight, people will come to you. You can't go into this business as an unformed designer or artist, you have to form yourself, wholly, and then the opportunities will follow.

The other thing to keep in mind is that you may not end up doing exactly what you went to school to do and you have to be open to those possibilities. I never knew I was a lighting designer, but I look back now and see many clues all through my life that were leading to that. You have to be open to where life can lead you because at the end of the path, you'll discover yourself. You have to be brave enough to travel down those unknown paths even if you don't know exactly where it will take you.

"You can't go into this business as an unformed designer or artist, you have to form yourself, wholly, and then the business will come to you."

HOWELL BINKLEY – LIGHTING DESIGNER
Saturday, May 21, 2011

Howell Binkley, who may best be know as a lighting designer and Tony Award-winner for his work on Jersey Boys, *is extremely passionate when it comes to training what he calls, "the next generation of Broadway's designers." He has recently developed a lighting internship through his Alma Mater, East Carolina University, through which young, eager student designers can come to New York City to work as an intern for Howell himself. As someone who firmly believes in practical experience as a means of fully understanding the art and craft of lighting design, Howell has been an ambassador to many young hopefuls as they begin their lighting design careers by working with him as either an assistant or an intern.*

He splits his time between projects regionally at theatres such as the La Jolla Playhouse, the Shakespeare Theatre in Washington DC, the Goodman Theatre, and the Hartford Stage, as well as many others. When he is not designing regionally, he is working out of his home in Harlem, New York on any number of Broadway and off-Broadway productions.

Howell is best recognized as a frequent collaborator with directors Hal Prince and Des McAnuff. In addition to his theatre designs, he is cofounder—along with his longtime friend and choreographer David Parsons—of the David Parsons Dance Company.

Q: So how did you get started in this profession?

A: It started at a very young age for me because the Business Agent for the IATSE was my next-door neighbor. I grew up in Winston Salem, North Carolina on a farm. As a young boy my parents would travel quite a bit so when they were gone, I would stay with my neighbors. When I stayed with them, my brother and I would go into the theatre and work. I would set up music stands for the symphony or work on the fly rail loading weight or lay a dance floor for Alvin Alley. Then, at night I would come back to the theatre wearing a coat and tie because we would be in charge of bringing the piano on and off the stage. I was only twelve years old, but I thought it was an awesome place to work and I loved the people, too. The other great thing was at the end of the day working at the theatre, they would pay me about twenty bucks so that wasn't bad either!

Once I got to high school I stayed really active backstage working on shows. During the summers, I would go to the North Carolina School of the Arts where they ran these intensive programs where high school students could go and learn about scenery, lighting, acting, directing, ballet; it covered everything and I absolutely loved all of it. I mean I was terrible in the dance classes and horrible at a lot of things, but I was really enjoying myself. That's really where my passion for the theatre began.

Q: Did you always know you wanted to be a lighting designer?

A: Actually, when I was young, I really wanted to be a mime. I actually got to study with Marcel Marceau and David Albert but obviously that career didn't pan out for me. I would literally go the malls in Winston Salem and work as a mime. I really wanted to be a performer and more specifically speaking, I really wanted to be Marcel Marceau. When I started college, I really wanted to become an architect but I couldn't get into the architecture school.

While I was in school at East Carolina University, I performed in a couple of plays, but it was really the dance department that caught my attention. The dance department wanted to present weekend performances to feature their dancers and choreographers. They contracted with the drama department to secure a small, repertory plot that consisted of about thirty instruments and one student designer. Now remember, this was back in the days of autotransformer dimmers where you had to use a broom handle to run the show! I had about eighteen dimmers, three boom positions, three side positions, and one color for all the backlight to work with and that's how I began as a lighting designer.

I would design around three dance pieces a month and soon it evolved into a pretty big deal on campus. We eventually turned it into a make shift Dinner Theatre, but it was dance. We set up tables and served food and beer and lit the tables as well as the performances. Some nights would feature jazz pieces, other nights featured ballet, and some nights it was modern dance and I would light the space accordingly. The other great thing was this was all run by the students–we did all of the technical and design work for the dance pieces so I really began to learn a lot just by doing it.

I was also pretty resourceful. In order to get more out of the lighting and since we were only given thirty instruments, I found a way to add lights without cutting into the inventory they would allow us to use. For some reason, our teachers didn't count the R40 strip lights in the thirty-instrument allotment, so I would surround the stage with strip lights just so I could have more design options. That's also where I really began to learn how to collaborate. I had to work with the choreographers and listen to what they needed and find a way to do it with a limited inventory and not a lot of time either.

Q: So how did you find yourself in a position to move to New York City?

A: What happened is that The Acting Company, which was run by John Houseman at that time, came to East Carolina and did a two-week residency on our campus, and I was able to meet their head electrician and work on their shows. After they left I received a call asking if I wanted to come and work with them during the summer in Saratoga, New York, which was their summer home. For $35 a week and a place to live and eat, I worked from 8:00 AM to midnight as an electrician. I would often go into the city with the truck drivers who would be picking up scenery or lighting equipment, so that was really how I was introduced to New York City.

I left college and moved to New York and began working at the John Houseman Acting Company where I assisted Dennis Parichy who was their resident lighting designer. I toured with them for about three years. We didn't even carry our own equipment, but we would go into a theatre and mount four shows using a repertory plot. We would take the scenery for the first show out, put down a new ground cloth, drop the electrics, change color, fly the electrics out and drop the new scenery in, and off we would go. That taught me so much about the importance of cuing. Working as Dennis's assistant was a major part of my development as a lighting designer. He taught me a lot and was another example of a great mentor.

Q: Is there a reason why you never went to graduate school?

A: Well to start with, I still lack six hours in order to receive my undergraduate degree. It's kind of strange because I go back to East Carolina to teach lighting and I still don't have my degree. In order for me to finish, I have to reapply. It's funny because this year when we opened *Lombardi* at Circle in the Square, I invited the Chancellor at ECU and his wife to attend the opening night performance because he is a huge football fan. He and his wife came, and in addition to seeing the show, they were able to meet Dave Robinson who was a Green Bay Packer between 1963 and 1972. After the show I joked with him saying, "Well, now can I get a degree?" We had a good laugh over that, but I still didn't get that degree!

Production photo, Howell Binkley Studio
West Side Story, 1st National Tour, 2010
Directed by Arthur Laurents
Lighting, Howell Binkley
Costumes, David C. Woolard
Set, James Youmans

Q: Can you talk a little bit about the importance of finding the right mentors and people to work with in this field?

A: Well, first of all, studying with Marcel Marceau and being able to learn a lot of technique and his values was absolutely wonderful. Another great thing that I am fortunate to have had in my life has been my opportunities to study with masters like Marcel Marceau, Hal Prince, and the great Arthur Laurents, who graciously wrote about me in his book. He was a true mentor.

I do have to say that it really was Hal Prince who put me on the map. He gave me my big break when he asked me to design *Kiss of the Spider Woman*. He saw an off-Broadway show I had done and his office called me. At the time, I thought someone was playing a practical joke on me. I had gotten a message on my beeper that was left by his longtime associate that said, "This is Ruth Mitchell from Hal Prince's office and Hal would like to meet with you." So I returned the call and arranged to meet with him at his office in a few days at 9:00 AM.

The night before that meeting I didn't sleep at all; I was scared to death. That morning, I got to his office in Rockefeller Center at around a quarter to nine. I met the secretary and said, "Hello. I'm Howell. I'm here to meet with Mr. Prince." She said, "OK fine. Would you like a cup of coffee?" "Sure," I said. And as I was sitting down in the waiting area, I heard this voice shout out from an office door that said, "Is Howell here?" And I said, "Yes." "Come on in," Hal said. So I went in and sat down. He said, "I saw that off-Broadway show and I really like your work. I understand you have a pretty solid reputation and I'm working on a new musical called *Kiss of the Spider Woman* and Jerome Sirlin is already on board to do the scenery and projections. Since you two have worked together I was wondering if you would be interested in lighting it." I said, "Yes Sir." He said, "Good. We will talk more soon. Goodbye." So, I was in his office for no more than ninety seconds in total; I hadn't even gotten my coffee yet and I had just landed my first Broadway show! So I have to give all the credit in the world to Mr. Hal Prince for putting me on the map. It's all about exposure in this industry.

Then, shortly after that show, Des McAnuff saw my work and now I work almost exclusively with Des. Then, Tommy Tune saw my work and we've established a great working relationship; these things just seem to escalate. Once you are on a streak and other people see your work and your craft, that's when you begin to create a name for yourself. I can honestly say that if it hadn't been for Hal, I really don't believe I would have had the opportunity to design some thirty Broadway shows that I've done since 1993.

I also met Jennifer Tipton while I was on the road working with Paul Taylor. She was their resident lighting designer, and I remember her telling me that I needed to get a company to design for because this one was hers. If I had to pick one person who was my primary mentor, it would be her. What I learned from her is immeasurable. She is a fabulous designer and wonderful mentor.

Q: What were you working on when Hal Prince found you?

A: I did a little James Joyce production with some of my acting company buddies on Theatre Row, when it used to be called Theatre Row, and Hal would go and see everything back then. After he saw that, he also saw another piece that I had worked on with the David Parson's Dance Company called *Caught*.

Now, the reason this piece was created was because at the time, both David Parsons and I worked for the Paul Taylor Company, where Jennifer Tipton was the resident lighting designer, and when we would create our seasons, Paul Taylor would often bring in a guest dancer to perform at one event in the season. In 1982, he happened to bring in Mikhail Baryshnikov. So, David, Mikhail, and I became quite close and we told him about this piece we wanted to do which was called *Caught*. At that time, the cost of the equipment was beyond what we could afford; we really didn't have any money. The next day, Mikhail handed me a check for $5,000 to get the strobe equipment with only one condition–he would be the first dancer to perform *Caught*. So, Mikhail performed it first, on the stage at the Met for their Board of Directors. It was an instant hit.

Q: How long had you been working away as a lighting designer in New York before you got your big break with *Kiss of the Spider Woman*?

A: It took about fifteen years before Hal Prince saw my work so there was plenty of work. I set a goal for myself, which was to have landed my first Broadway show by the time I was thirty years old; Unfortunately, I was about ten years off.

Q: Is it the work you enjoy the most or is it the relationships you get to create and develop that keeps you hungry?

A: I've been very fortunate as a designer and I recognize that every day. I'm fortunate to have worked with the people I've worked with and do the projects that I am doing. I can also say that it's not because I am the best designer there is out there. It's because of the relationships I've cultivated over the past, how-ever-many years it's been.

My good friend David Parsons and I started a dance company over twenty years ago and it's still going strong today. We employ eleven full-time dancers who work fifty-two weeks a year, and they are covered from head to toe as far as insurance is concerned. To be completely honest with you, that is what I love to do. I believe in serving as an inspiration to the younger generations of designers and other performing artists if it is at all possible. I know there are a lot of wonderful lighting designers out there who are also great colleagues of mine. This business is really about creating and cultivating strong relationships with artists that you connect with and love to work with day after day. The work is great, but we spend an awful lot of time doing it, and if you don't like the people you are working with that can be a big problem.

Q: Other than talent and craft, what do you look for when you hire assistant designers?

A: It's all about what you bring into the room, and that involves so much more than technical and design skills. The group of young associate designers who work with me have all been carefully selected; I am meticulous as to who I choose to work with, and it's not just based on their talent. Their personality and how they are perceived when they walk into a room is also very important.

When I have to leave the tech table during a rehearsal to take a call or whatever it may be, I know the director of that particular show can turn to any of my associates and say, "That cue was a bit too fast." Or they can say, "Can we brighten that area down stage left just a bit?" Some designers don't allow associates to take and execute the notes, whereas I really treat my associates as team members. I think that's one thing that I am very, very happy to be able to do in my career. They really have to learn and this is how it's done. I also let them focus my shows. I will give them the notes and let them work them through so they understand what it takes to work with a union crew and work within a specific framework of time–it's absolutely the only way they will begin to learn how to function once they get out on their own. I will also go to bat for my associates when needed. I've been in situations where production technical directors will say to me, "Well, usually we don't have the associate designers do notes. That's the designers job." And I will let them know that, if they are going to have me work with them, this is how I like to work. I want my associates to understand exactly what we are doing and to fully understand that, they have to be a part of everything.

I am fanatical about finding ways to bring young students to this city so they can begin to see how great a life in the theatre can be. I have one young lady who has assisted me on seven Broadway shows and she's twenty-six years old. They really are the future of this business and it's really all about exposure, which is why I am so passionate about bringing young assistants into a Broadway theatre

"It's all about what you bring into the room and that involves so much more than technical and design skills."

so they can work with me and see what it's like. Every assistant who works with me is introduced to the director. I think it's critical to train the next generation in ways that accurately represent what life is really like in a commercial theatre. They need to be encouraged to have the courage to make the leap to come to New York and just "wing" it. Sometimes you have to jump in the deep end with your pants on!

Q: Do you think it is important that young designers establish a style, and if so, what is your style when it comes to identifying your lighting?

A: I try to establish an aerial signature with my lighting. To me it's not about the lighting as a separate entity, it's about what you light, how it's lit, and how you execute your cueing. That's what's really important to me. Cueing is a very serious aspect of lighting a show. There are some shows that tend to be "over-cued" and it can wear out the audience. When the space is sculpted and textured with subtle cueing, it can be absolutely stunning.

When I light musicals, there may be LED screens and chase sequences for emphasis in musical numbers, and all of that is wonderful and exciting, but when the book scenes begin, I try very hard to create intimacy and focus on the actors, while still paying attention to the surrounding space that lives within that proscenium arch. I think that "negative space" that surrounds the actor is very important to compose as well as what plays on the actors. You really have to carve into the space with your cuing and then at the right moments, take the light away for the transitions. Once the transition into the new cue is complete, it's the lighting designers job to reestablish the new moment, once again, through cuing. I've really learned how to fine-tune my cuing by working with great choreographers and great directors.

I also believe that my work has evolved as the technology has evolved. Now, with these 3-D digital models the set designers create, I am able to walk through the entire show with a director to show them exactly what I am thinking moment by moment. That is what I refer to as "formatting" the show. The set model is a wonderful tool to use with a director to format the show so you don't have to walk into the theatre on that first tech, naked, not having discussed the lighting possibilities ahead of time.

Q: Do you approach a lighting design differently when you work in a space like Circle in the Square, since it is a theatre in the round?

A: Absolutely. You have to because you really have to carve out your areas so the audience that is sitting all the way around the stage can

Production photo, Anna Louizos Studio
In the Heights, Richard Rodgers Theatre, New York NY, 2008
Directed by Thomas Kail
Lighting, Howell Binkley
Costumes, Paul Tazewell
Set, Anna Louizos

have a similar stage picture. When you dissect your stage and develop your acting areas, you have to realize that instead of only two lights into an area, now there needs to be six because you don't want the actor to turn and be in the dark for half of your audience. You really have to approach the sculpting in a different way. You also have to be careful about color selection because you don't have traditional back-light because one side of the audience's backlight is another side of the audience's front light, so it can get a bit tricky.

I was lucky on *Lombardi* because it featured a ring of white lights that visually symbolized the traditional football stadium light-ing, but it was also my saving grace because it was great front fill light for every area. That decision came down to great collaboration, too. The set designer and the director realized that what we wanted to do originally was far too expensive for our budget, so we decided that the next best approach was this single ring of lighting.

We actually teched that show up in Massachusetts in a tra-ditional, proscenium theatre so I actually had an entire upstage wall of somewhere in the count of 200 par cans to accomplish what we did with a single ring of par cans once we got to Circle in the Square.

We also workshopped the show when it was up in Massachusetts and we did that so all of the designers and the director could establish the vocabulary for the show. We knew it was going to go land at Circle in the Square, so we all thought, "Well, at least we can work out the tour version here."

When we finally moved to Circle in the Square, I set up my tech table at one end of the house for the first work through of the show. Once we got all the way through, I moved the tech table to the other end of the theatre to watch it from that vantage point to make sure it looked the way we needed it to look. For each of the four weeks of tech, I moved my table to all four sides of that space to make sure we did our job properly. I got to see it from every angle and I wanted to make sure that those audience members, no matter where they sat, got the show I wanted them to see.

Q: When there is a projection designer on a project that you are lighting, how do you deal with the fact that you no longer are in control of the brightest light source on the stage?

A: It's all about focus. You can never let loose of the story that's being told of that musical or play. It's a very integral and delicate marriage between the two. *Jersey Boys* has a lot of wonderful projections where the collaboration between Michael Clark and myself had to be absolutely in sync with one another. The thing that has to remain the focus of any designer is to not lose focus on the story that is being told. I guess that's where my old fashioned approach comes into play, but that's what I learned from people like Hal Prince and Des McAnuff. Every note I got was tied to the story that we were all trying to tell. There are times when a designer wants to exploit their craft, but if it ends up blurring the story, it cannot happen.

Back in 1986, Jennifer Tipton gave me my first regional work at American Repertory Theatre to redo her design for *Alcestis*, which Robert Wilson had directed, and soon after working with him on that production I began doing a number of shows with him. And it's all thanks to Jennifer for allowing me that kind of exposure. I had put in enough time with her to where she recognized I was ready, and I took full advantage of that opportunity.

Q: When did you join the Union?

A: Well, it took me five times to get in! The strange thing was, I was a working designer and each year I would go to take the exam, I wouldn't pass. I was either on the road with Paul Taylor or The Acting Company, or doing rock and roll shows, and every year when

I would come back to take the test, they would say, "Oh, you're back again." Looking back on it now, it's funny, but boy, that was frustrating. After I finally got my card, a few years later I sat on the exam committee and I was a complete hard ass when it came to those designers trying to get in! I think it was my retribution.

Q: Did you make a conscious choice to try to work on Broadway rather than off-Broadway when you first started out?

A: No, not at all. Back then, and even today, I will design anything that comes my way. The reality was, after I landed *Kiss of the Spider Woman*, my career on Broadway just took off. Hal Prince put me on the map, and it was his trust and generosity that made my career catapult to the next level in an instant, and for that I cannot thank him enough. I recognized that it was an amazing break for my career so I took advantage of it. Most of the off-Broadway work I had done before that was as an assistant or as an electrician. I was doing everything I could to make enough money to pay my bills.

Q: How did you manage the financial demands of New York City when you were first starting off?

A: I was really lucky. Back in 1979 when I first got here, I found this tiny place on 14th Street that was only about $500 a month. It allowed me to go to places like Production Arts and work for whatever they could pay me. Back then the social scene here in New York was also very unified when it came to the stagehands. There was one little bar that all of us would go and hang out at and talk shop. If I needed work, I knew if I went there, I probably could get on a call and make enough money to pay some bills. We also looked out for one another, too; it was a tight little community of theatre technicians and designers.

Q: How would people describe working with Howell Binkley?

A: It's all about what you bring to the room as a designer and a human being. That is critical in this business. Your organization, your personality, your ability to be on time, your excitement; those are key elements to me and I preach those things to the young assistants who work with me. I want them to look good, dress well, they need to show up to meetings and work calls on time, they have to bring excitement, and they need to shake hands with everyone they meet and greet them. That kind of behavior and attitude is key to me because I am kind of a "good ole southern boy." A respectful attitude and appearance helps the stagehands and all of the other collaborators in the room all feel part of an ensemble. I think a lot of directors respond to that about me and that's why they like me to be in the room. It's attitude, passion, and personality that will get you the second job. There can be some really difficult people to work with in this business and I never want to be that guy. I want people to be happy and excited to see me instead of dreading what I may say to them or ask them to do.

I also think it's our responsibility to instill those attitudes in the next generation of designers, because one day it will be in their hands. I firmly believe that it's our responsibility to help train them to be wonderful peer collaborators and artists. Whether you're working in a regional theatre environment or in New York at the Helen Hayes Theatre or in a university setting, a positive, collaborative attitude and a respectful demeanor are required.

Q: Do you think you will ever move into the realm of academia as a teacher of lighting design?

A: What I have learned about myself is that I am a pretty horrible teacher when it comes to the classroom, but if you can get me in a theatre with a group of young designers, that's a completely different story. I think that's actually OK because it's in the theatre where they really begin to learn what this industry is all about anyway. You can teach your butt off in a classroom, but until you are in the theatre, in that environment where the pressure of the schedule with all of the deadlines and the reality of the budget is right in front of you, you really haven't experienced the truth about this business. It's something that just doesn't translate in the classroom–it only happens in the theatre. When I get students to sit at a tech table, in the theatre, and see the way I execute and the speed at which I work, that's where I am most comfortable "teaching." The difference between the classroom and the theatre is night and day.

> **"Whether you're working in a regional theatre environment or in New York at the Helen Hayes Theatre or in a university setting, a positive, collaborative attitude and a respectful demeanor are required."**

Production photo, Howell Binkley Studio
Baby It's You!, Broadhurst Theatre, New York NY, 2011
Directed by Floyd Mutrux and Sheldon Epps
Lighting, Howell Binkley
Costumes, Lizz Wolf
Set, Anna Louizos

Q: When a young lighting designer is faced with a large production, what advice would you give him or her?

A: It's all about what I mentioned before which is in the "formatting" of the show. It's about the time you spend dissecting the show long before you get into the theatre. Another critical component of the lighting designer's ability to function effectively once he or she gets to the theatre is to attend as many rehearsals as possible. That's probably one of the most key things I preach to my assistants; you have to go to rehearsals. There may be some days when you will sit in that rehearsal room for eight hours while they work on one scene over and over and over again, but you need to be there so you can learn the vocabulary of the room.

You're also there so you can learn about the actors and they can also get to know you as well. You begin to create a familiarity between yourself and the performers. I've worked with a lot of actors who tell me how comfortable they are on stage in the light that I am creating. To me, that's one of the highest complements you can get as a lighting designer. When the performer is comfortable and knows where they are supposed to be on stage in order to be in the proper light, their performance will be the best it can possibly be. When they're in tune with your cueing in a subconscious way, where they feel the subtle changes as well as the bumps at the end of numbers, that's when everything falls into place and becomes one. I couldn't do that if I didn't spend hours upon hours in the rehearsal room learning their movement and what I call the vocabulary of the piece. Building that trust between the actor and the director is so very important—I can't stress that enough. Put the time in during rehearsals and it will pay off once you get at that tech table to write the cues. It's especially critical for my associates who train the production follow spot operators. I want them to be in rehearsal every day so they already have their cue sheets made to give to the follow spot operators once we move into the theatre. Of course, once we get to the theatre there will be adjustments to the type of spot whether it's a full body pick up or a head or head and waist or soft or hard focus; but, for all intents and purposes, the cue sheets are done. Attending as many rehearsals as possible is vital to any lighting designer, regardless of your experience or talent.

Also, a young person should realize that the word "can't" should not exist in his or her vocabulary. If a director wants a person to be standing down left and it's too dark, it's my job to accommodate that request. Even when inventory is limited, I still have to make his or her vision a reality. It's not for me to say, "Well, if you moved that actor eighteen inches stage left, there is better light there." My job is to give the director what they asked for in all situations and that's the attitude I try to instill in my assistants as well. If they ask me the question, "Would it help you Howell if the actor moved two feet down stage?" I would say, "Sure, that would be great." But the word "can't" isn't in my vocabulary. Now, if the reality of my inventory is such that the sky is NOT the limit, it then comes down to communication with that director and ultimately, the formatting I do in order to maximize my options. It's always about options. If I can provide options for a director, it makes both of our lives much easier.

Q: Does your artistic vision change when you are faced with a tighter budget production for, let's say, off-Broadway or for a regional theatre?

A: That's a great question and one that is difficult to answer. Because the audiences have become accustomed to such a high caliber of execution, it ultimately comes down to the dollar and the weekly and what is available. Even when there's not the budget we would like to have, it's still my job to come up with a creative solution that doesn't end up compromising the integrity of the show. Also, if it is a regional theatre or a smaller venue, I can call in a favor to a rental house that I am familiar with and get them to donate equipment or offer it at a reduced price, which often times will be exactly what we need. You just have to find a creative solution without compromising the integrity of the production.

Q: If a young designer asked you about the life of a freelance designer, how would you describe it?

A: Well, to be honest, it's been quite a rollercoaster of a life, that's for sure. There have been ups and probably just as many downs, but that's what this life is all about! Something that was really helpful for me was that I didn't have student loans when I moved to New York. That allowed me a certain kind of financial and artistic freedom that, at the time, I took for granted.

I actually didn't even think about the lifestyle of a freelance designer; I just went for it. I just kept living week to week. There were times when things were really slow and I had to go to my friends and ask them for money so I could eat or pay my rent. Then, when I would have a really good week, I would pay them back. I guess it boils down to the fact that I just knew that this was where I wanted to be and what I wanted to do so I did anything and everything to make it happen—I was going to make it work.

The great thing is, I'm not finished. I still have a long way to go! I'm happy where I'm at, but for me, there's no light at the end of the tunnel yet. I am going to keep moving forward always looking for that next gig, and I do that through relationships. I do that by staying in connection with the choreographers, writers, composers and directors I've met and have had the pleasure to work with over the last twenty years. It may sound naïve, but I just went for it and I haven't had the sense to stop going for it to this day!

Q: It sounds like you really enjoy working with young designers?

A: I absolutely do. What I really like to do is bring young students here to New York so they can be exposed to what goes on in and around the theatre. I will bring young people from La Jolla, Chicago, Washington, and all over the country here so they can really begin to understand what it takes to be a working designer. And the only way they can fully understand it is to experience it. Right now I am working with three very talented, young designers up in Stratford and they are wonderful. They are the future; they are the new generation of designers and I feel some responsibility to share what I know with them so they begin to grasp what it will take in order for them to make it in this incredibly difficult business.

Some of them will tell me how scared they are to make the move to New York City and my response has been simply this: Come

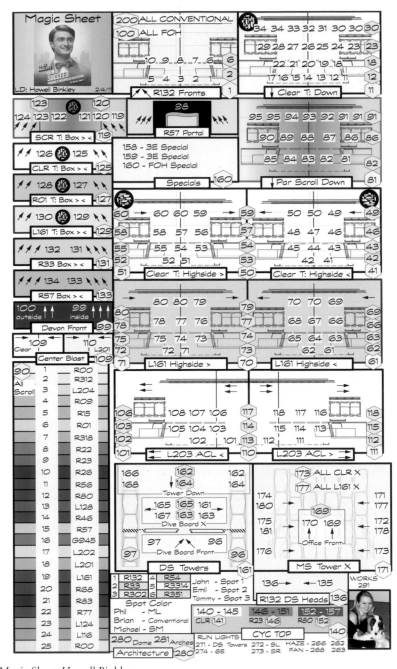

Magic Sheet, Howell Binkley
How to Succeed in Business Without Really Trying, Al Hirschfeld Theatre, New York, NY, 2011

to the city, stay here for a while, and work with me. I will do all I can to show you how to make the best of your talents and ambitions.

I also started a scholarship back at East Carolina University where we help young designers afford the opportunity to come to New York City and work as an intern in my office. This is where it all happens and that's not to say you can't be successful in other cities like Chicago or Dallas or Atlanta, because you certainly can. But, if you want to work in New York City, you have to be in New York City.

Q: What final piece of advice do you have for young designers?

A: I urge my assistants to read the New York Times. I will often ask them, "Do you read the paper?" And their response is generally, "Well, we look at it on the computer every now and then." And my response is always, "No. Pick up the paper and get some ink on your fingers!" Maybe I'm old fashioned, but I think they need to pick that paper up and read about who is designing where, and what new shows are coming up, and what theatres are premiering new work. This is our industry and I guess I believe there's something to picking up the newspaper and reading about our peers and the work they are creating; that's still very important.

I totally understand the importance of the computer and all of its beauty in how we communicate, but I relate to a physical paper in the same way I relate to a physical light plot that I draw. I still think there's something to be said about drafting a plot by hand on onionskin paper. Today what happens is that I will sit down with my associates and talk about the plot with them. They will then take that plot and draft it into the computer. Then, the next day, we will look at a computer print out of the plot that shows us the available real estate for our equipment, but I will still get my pencil out and draw on it making notes about space, or instrumentation, or position, or any other changes we see needed. I still have to get my fingers dirty. Then, they take that back, make all of the changes in the computer, and we start all over again until it's exactly what we want.

Q: What is one of the best things about being a lighting designer?

A: To me it's the room. I love being creative with people I enjoy being around.

Howell Binkley

DAVID LANDER – LIGHTING DESIGNER
Saturday, February 12, 2011

My conversation with David Lander took place in the heart of the theatre district at his studio, located above the Helen Hayes Theatre on West 44th Street. David had just wrapped up technical rehearsals for Bengal Tiger at the Bagdad Zoo *starring Robin Williams and was in the very early planning stages of the upcoming Broadway revival of Terrence McNally's* Master Class.

Although David made his first appearance as a Broadway designer during the late 1990s, it was the Tony Award-winning Broadway hit 33 Variations *from the 2009 season that seemed to propel David into a new category of highly sought-after lighting designers. David works extensively not only in New York but across the United States in regional theatres such as the Mark Taper Forum in Los Angeles and the Alley Theatre in Houston. He has also worked overseas in Japan, Greece, Singapore, Australia, London, and Caracas to name a few places.*

Aside from live theatre and opera, David has also worked in film, dance, and architectural lighting, and has designed numerous special events. He has served as one of the resident lighting designers at the MUNY theatre in Saint Louis, Missouri for ten seasons. David has been nominated for Drama Desk Awards for his work on Dirty Blonde *and* I Am My Own Wife *and received the Drama Desk for* Bengal Tiger at the Bagdad Zoo. *He has also received two Tony nominations for his contribution to 33* Variations *and* Bengal Tiger.

Q: How did you initially become interested in theatre?

A: As a Cub Scout, we had to complete special projects to achieve merit beads. On the list was to put on a puppet show. So I enrolled my father to help me build a theatre and my friends to help put on the show. My grandmother was the first audience I had. She seemed to like the show! I expanded the theatre and gathered more friends. We continued performing through high school as the "No Name Puppet Theatre" company. We performed at birthday parties, parks and recreation centers, one time at a country club's swimming pool. We would customize a show to whoever would hire us. I wrote the scripts, built the puppets and the theatre, marketed the company, produced, etc. It was a lot of fun and I learned a lot. We had a simple lighting system, cans with colored light bulbs. Red, blue, green, white and black light bulbs! The colored lights were controlled with on/off switches and the white light was on a dimmer. I enjoyed creating mood and special lighting effects for the shows. I always wanted more lights and better control.

The puppets led me to want to study both performance and design. I was equally interested in both on stage as well as what went on back stage. I think when I was in tenth grade I knew I wanted to study theatre in college. When I started to look at colleges, my parents wanted me to have a practical and sensible career so I began searching for schools that had a good computer science program, as well as a good theatre program. I was looking for schools that had solid liberal arts programs and a theatre program that had good physical facilities. I wanted a school that produced big shows on big stages.

I ended up going to the Ohio State University for undergraduate studies. My parents thought I was enrolling in computer science, but during my first month of classes I changed my major from computer science to theatre. Since both departments were in the College of Arts and Sciences, the switch was easy. I did continue with computer science for almost two years, but the theatre courses became too intensive and I dropped the computer classes.

In addition to course requirements, I took as many electives as possible. I stayed an additional quarter, as I was given a main-stage show to design, which was a bid deal as an undergraduate. I studied French, art history, painting and drawing, in addition to the required courses, and of course computer science. I took an incredible class in color theory that was in the art department. It's so important to become as well rounded as you can during your undergraduate studies while taking theatre and design courses. As an undergraduate student you will learn theatre craft. Graduate school is where you will specialize and refine your talents and learn the art. Don't get me wrong, you will learn theatre art in undergrad; however, I cannot stress enough the importance of a well-rounded undergraduate degree—study as much as you can.

> **"As an undergraduate student you will learn theatre craft. Graduate school is where you will specialize and refine your talents and learn the art."**

Q: Where did you go to graduate school?

A: I attended NYU for graduate school. My primary mentor while I was at NYU was the late John Gleason.

Q: Be honest—what's it like being a designer in New York City?

A: It's tough here in New York. It's really tough to make a living as a freelance designer.

Q: Why is it so difficult?

A: That is a graduate school class that would take a year to teach. "How to make it in New York." Paying the rent. Putting food on the table. I know those are basic needs, but add paying back student loans into that equation and if you are not careful and don't pay your estimated income tax (for work on 1099 based fees) you will be paying back taxes for last year as well as current taxes. Staring out in your career, it's hard work to get your "first break." Knocking on doors and paying your dues are somewhat of a cliché, but true nevertheless. You have to start off slow and build your network of friends and acquaintance, and invest time and effort to cultivate relationships with directors and choreographers by designing off-off Broadway and assisting at the same time.

When you design a show it falls under one of two categories. There's commercial theatre and there's not-for-profit. I would say roughly 90 percent of the theatre that is out there is not-for-profit theatre. But the real earning potential comes from working in the commercial theatre. For-profit theatre, or commercial theatre, is essentially where the box office funds the production in its entirety. If you don't sell tickets, the show closes. Big money is behind most commercial shows. With big money comes concern over who is going to deliver a quality product, relating to the creative team. It takes time to develop a name in order to be trusted to design on a show that has a lot at stake, i.e. producers who have invested millions.

Q: What kind of financial investment are we talking about for a Broadway show?

A: Plays cost approximately between two and three million dollars and musicals cost approximately seven to fifteen million dollars. That's a large sum of money. The way shows generate money is with ticket sales and the producers want to begin performances as quickly as possible; however, the creative team wants as much time as possible in technical rehearsals. There's always an urgent need to tech the

Production photo, David Lander
Falstaff, Julliard Opera, Peter Jay Sharp Theatre, New York NY, 2009
Directed by Stephen Wadsworth
Lighting, David Lander
Costumes, Sam Fleming
Set, Derek McLane

show as quickly and efficiently as possible, because as they say, "time is money." Designers are hired based on their art, talent, and speed at which they can maneuver through a challenging tech process under stress, and make the production look great.

There is an adrenalin rush that is involved in being a lighting designer. The lighting designer is the last member of the design team to be able to physically work on the production, and it can only happen in the theatre; therefore, it is a very public process. The set designer builds the model in their studio and the costume designer sketches in the privacy of their studio, but the lighting designer doesn't get that luxury. A lighting designer's work is done in the theatre with everyone watching and the entire cast and crew waiting, but I digress. Ultimately, we are hired to be good as well as fast.

Q: Is there any way to come out ahead, financially, as a designer?

A: In commercial theatre, because of the structure of the finances, aside from the fee we are paid, we are also paid a "royalty." This is paid weekly after the first public performance. In television and motion pictures it's sometimes called a "residual." Every time a sitcom rerun is aired on television, the actor gets a payment. Every time a song is played on the radio, the singer gets a "royalty." Likewise, in a commercial venture, be it Broadway or Stars on Ice, or any other 100 percent commercial venture, you will be able to negotiate a "royalty" for your contribution. This money is what enables designers to rise above just making ends meet. When you get enough shows running and the royalties are plentiful, you are then able to hire an accountant and invest this money for retirement, maybe even buy an apartment or house. There are some off-Broadway theatres that are commercial as well, so they are included in this category.

Q: Give me an example of a completely commercial show that many of us would be familiar with?

Phantom of the Opera, Wicked, Cats, Les Miserables, Lion King to name a few. Getting hired on a show as successful as *Phantom of the Opera* is the designer's dream. Landing a long running show that has multiple companies running worldwide, where each company pays a royalty to the designer is the ultimate in commercial success. When a designer gets a successful show, I use a metaphor of Holden Caulfield's sister Phoebe as she grabs the "golden ring" while riding the merry-go-round in "Catcher in the Rye." Catch the golden ring and you win a prize. The prize in this instance is financial security. There are very few designers who get the big shows that are lucrative in the likes of a *Les Miserables* or *Phantom of the Opera*.

Q: It's like owning a patent on a product; only the product is your design, right?

A: Yes. We license our design to the production. Every performance, we get paid for the use of our designs, which are our ideas, or "Intellectual property." In fact, Congress is passing new legislation on what "Intellectual Property" actually means. For example, on the Internet, people are copying and distributing films and TV shows and this is an example of copyright infringement. Laws are needed to protect piracy. But that's another conversation.

Q: Do all commercial ventures operate this way or are there exceptions?

A: There are some exceptions. For instance, there are certain companies and projects that assign you as a "work for hire" employee. You don't get any participation in the profits. You sign a contract that is either based on an hourly, daily, or weekly rate. If for instance, the movie goes on to be a huge blockbuster, you will not share any of the profits. But don't get me wrong; the fees are pretty good in these areas. Fees are regulated by union contracts, which govern base rates, or minimums that producers must pay. We like when we get paid more than the minimum, and the unions do their best to negotiate fair minimums. In theatre, lighting designers fall under the union United Scenic Artists.

Q: So, should a young person even consider going into this field since it is so seemingly difficult to earn a living?

A: "Should a young person consider being a freelance lighting designer as a profession?" I guess my answer is, don't do it if you want to make a lot of money. It takes time a long time to grab the "Golden Ring." For shows like *Cats, Phantom, Les Miserables,* and a handful of others, the designers who make those weekly fees are participating in the ultimate profit sharing theatre experience. If money is your biggest goal, I would say no—choose another path. If you love theatre and can't imagine doing anything else with your life, then yes, the theatre is an exciting place to work.

Q: How do you go about that process of hiring assistant designers?

A: Most simply, I find assistants through word of mouth. A young designer coming to New York first off should find an internship. An internship can lead to becoming an assistant in that same studio, which will help to simplify the interview process. You will have to interview to get an internship, but the requirements are less stringent. The reality of this city is that when you first arrive here, the shows that you are going to be able to qualify to design are going to be on small, not-for-profit productions. These theatres usually don't have very big budgets, so you will end up being the designer, electrician, and the programmer. You will probably be asked to hang the show, focus the show, and cue the show all for maybe one hundred dollars. That, however, will have to be your night job. You cannot survive on $100 a week. Your day job is what you use to pay the rest of your bills. As an assistant you could make between $18 and $40 per hour, depending on your skills. I know of some design assistants who work on TV and films and make upwards of $65 per hour, which is certainly more than designing an entire show for one hundred dollars. You can also work as an electrician off and off-off Broadway; however, I caution young designers who take that route. You may become known as an electrician instead of a designer, which is why it is better, in my opinion, to work as an assistant designer.

Q: Do assistant lighting designers need to be in the United Scenic Artists Union in order to work in New York?

A: In order to work for a designer who is working on a Broadway show, you must be in the Union (USA-829). Some other non-Broadway venues,

Production photo, David Lander Studio
Séance on a Wet Afternoon, Opera Santa Barbara, 2009
Directed by Scott Schwartz
Lighting, David Lander
Costumes, Alejo Vietti
Set, Heidi Ettinger

such as the Metropolitan Opera, Carnegie Hall, and Lincoln Center, also require assistants to be in USA-829. Regionally, there are a few places across the country where you need to be a union member, like the MUNY in St. Louis and the LA Opera to name a few. I guess the rule is, if the theatre employs IATSE stagehands, most likely everyone working in that theatre will need to be on a Union contract, including the assistants. In regional theatre, the designer must be in the Union, and if he or she is not, they are only allowed to design three shows before having to join the union; however, the rules aren't as strict for the assistants.

Q: Do you ever get inquires from young designers who would like to work with you as an assistant and if so, how do you handle those unsolicited requests?

A: I am always flattered when someone emails or writes me. I try to respond to everybody. I remember when I was just out of grad school and the many people who didn't return my phone calls. We didn't have emails back in the early 1990s; I mean we did, but I didn't. I would write letters and make phone calls to people I thought were amazing designers, and I would arrange to meet with them. Even though I may not have gotten the job, I still considered it a valuable opportunity just to have met with them. So now, when people contact me, I do my best to respond to everyone and meet as many of them as possible. When I meet them, I try to make it clear that I may not have work right now, and they should keep in touch. If I don't have work for them, I can sometimes suggest other studios for them to consider visiting. I tell people to bring drafting in addition to a photographic portfolio. I want to see their body of work. I want to ascertain their skill level, but ultimately I want to see their drafting. Initially, I am going to hire them to draft. I also make a point to ask them to bring something hand drafted.

Q: Why do you ask designers to bring hand drafting, since almost everyone in the theatre industry is computer drafting?

A: Quite simply, I want to see their lettering. I am a stickler for lettering. I also expect my assistants to be able to do a hand drawn sketch. It used to be that we would create a sketch and fax or mail it out. We don't do that anymore. Now it is a quick sketch, a scan, and then an email, but it is pretty much the same thing. I may have an assistant hand letter a label on a CD or a file cover as part of a presentation. It then becomes a representation of my studio and I want it to look great.

Also, hand drafting illustrates your ability to organize. It's very easy to draft on a computer, because you can delete and nudge and move. When you draft a light plot by hand, you will start with a large blank piece of paper. You have to organize your drawing in your head before you put pencil to paper and draw centerline and plaster line. How are you going to lay out that piece of paper? Or, if you are drawing a piece of scenery that has multiple views, you need to know whether the scenic piece has more stuff stage right, or more stuff stage left, so you will adjust the center line on the piece of paper accordingly. It's a blank piece of paper that's a thought process and ultimately, a design process. Those kinds of details are really important to me.

A few years ago, I interviewed a talented young designer for an assistant position. As always, I got to the part of the interview where I asked to see something hand drafted. He pulled out a large light plot completely drafted by hand. Something I don't see any more. I was even more impressed to find out he had prepared the plot solely for the interview. Needless to say, he got the job. It is important to go that extra step–you always have to go that extra step.

Q: What size staff do you try to keep?

A: I usually have one person working with me at a time, and it is on a show-by-show basis. I would love to have a full time design assistant and a part-time administrative assistant as well, to keep me organized, but mainly it is one person per show. I have several assistants that I like to work with as our schedules coordinate. Since I cannot keep any one person 100 percent employed, they have to take other work either assisting or designing their own productions. So when one assistant is not available, I will call another. When none of my regulars are available, I will look through the résumé file and call someone who recently interviewed, or ask one of my assistants who they would recommend.

Q: Is there a concern that when you come to New York and begin working as an assistant, you could be pigeon holed into that role for the rest of your career, as opposed to being considered for design jobs?

A: In lighting design, I don't think that happens. You can control how you are viewed. After grad school, I started assisting. I was assisting solidly for several years until I was able to get good design jobs. As I mentioned earlier, you may have to keep assisting to support yourself until the design jobs are able to financially pay all the bills. I was designing, but I also continued to assist for about five more years. During that period, I lit my first Broadway production, but I still needed to assist to help pay the bills. You will have to make a conscious choice to stop assisting or you could become stuck in that place, not necessarily "pigeon holed."

Q: So is getting an MFA important since so much is learned on the job?

A: Absolutely. School is essential. At the grad school level it's mostly theoretical (paper projects). When you work for someone you will learn the business and there's really no other way to learn that side of this industry. As you are assisting, it's important to absorb as much as you can and also ask questions. Then, you start meeting other assistants and other assistant directors and you begin to network. That network is critical, because it's made up of associate set designers, associate choreographers and associate directors; those are the people who will become your friends. Those are the people you need to stay in close contact with, because in five or ten years, those are the people you will be working with.

The other transition you will experience is the pay cut you go through when you transition from assisting to designing. When you're assisting, you earn a weekly salary. When you're a designer, you get a fee. If you are on a USA contract as an assistant, it's a weekly salary. Assistants can end up making more money than the designer. In a commercial theatre venture, if it's a hit (and we want all shows to be a hit!) then the royalty checks will begin and make up the financial difference.

Q: Is it possible to take multiple shows in order to offset the income problem?

A: As a lighting designer, it's difficult. Set designers can do multiple shows at a time; whereas, lighting designers can do one at a time, which usually works out to be about one show per month. It comes down to this, when you are hired to light the show, the producer is expecting you to be there. They're not expecting your assistant to do it because you are off working on another project. They hired you and your ideas.

Q: Do you advise young people to join the union right away when they move to New York?

A: You cannot just join the Union. You have to apply and be admitted under recommendation of your peers and/or take a union exam. For lighting designers, the exam consists of completing a paperwork project and an interview. The paperwork project tests your design skills in generating a plot and paperwork under a time constraint. The interview portion of the exam is a review of your portfolio. To create your portfolio you have to have either worked as a designer or have completed an educational program in which you have had shows produced. New, inexperienced designers coming to New York probably are not going to be designing on Broadway immediately; however, if you want to be a designer or assistant designer on Broadway, you must be in the Union. If you're interested in working as a draftsperson or studio assistant, then you don't have to be in the Union. One major benefit that the Union provides is participation in the pension and welfare funds. Pension is the retirement program and welfare is the health insurance program. To qualify for both you have to generate a certain minimum amount of money on union contracts. Having health care is a valuable part of any business plan.

Q: It sounds daunting. The idea of coming to New York to begin a life in the theatre seems like it is wrought with pitfalls. If it is so difficult, why are you still here? Is it to land that big hit . . . grab that "Gold Ring?"

A: I love theatre. I love live performance. Being in the same room as the performers and the audience and watching the chemistry as they interact. I haven't been fortunate yet to have a long-running show. So

Production photo, David Lander Studio
The Clean House, Cincinnati Playhouse in the Park, Cincinnati, OH, 2006
Directed by Michael Haney
Lighting, David Lander
Costumes, Gordon DeVinney
Set, Narelle Sissons

there is a concept called "quality of life." That's ultimately the decision-making factor on how you spend your career. When you choose to move to New York or California or Arkansas, your quality of life, as well as your career, is going to be different in each of those locations. New York is expensive. Los Angeles is also pretty expensive. Chicago isn't as expensive, and I would assume that Fayetteville, AR is even less expensive. It's all about choices and opportunities. Do you want to have five roommates while you're living in New York starting your career? If you want to have any chance of keeping your bills down, you have to make these kinds of choices—eventually it all comes back to finances. They sometimes force you into making career choices.

Q: So how is your "quality of life?" Are you living the life you want?

A: There is nothing else like designing for the theatre. I get to play "make believe" every day and get paid for it! That's why we get into this field, right? That's why we're artists. We need an outlet for our creativity. We are also pretty crazy. You have to be a little bit nuts to do this type of work, because it certainly isn't a nine to five job. You are always looking for the next job as a freelance designer. If you want a steady, nine to five job, this is not the field for you.

Q: Is there anywhere a designer can work if he or she wants a more structured life?

A: Of course. There are many design studios that have staff and a structure that is more corporate. Studios such as Disney hire illustrators and graphic artists, or Pixar hires animators, for instance. There are also a number of other companies, like NBC or HBO, where you could find a nine to five job drafting, shopping, researching, etc. Or, you could work for a sitcom or daytime television, but the show might get canceled, so there really isn't a lot of stability in that line of work either, as I think about it. You may have to go to work for a company like IBM to get job security–there is no security as a freelance designer. You have to make your own security; and it's not for everyone. You have to sell yourself and be extremely motivated to work as a freelance designer because, as I said at the very beginning of this interview, you have to be able to put food on the table, and that is something you don't learn in school.

Q: There is a saying, "You never get a second chance to make a first impression." How important is it for a young person to make a positive "first impression" when he or she meets a designer?

A: I hear what you're saying, of course first impressions are telling, but talent is what it's all about. If I meet someone who is talented and they unintentionally say something or do something inappropriate, I can still see the talent in that person. If someone brings their portfolio to me and their drafting isn't up to par, but I can see that they are talented, I will urge them to go and get a bit more experience. Work on the drafting. I will most certainly urge them to come back again and see me.

Q: How does someone get work if they don't know anyone in the business?

A: It's very hard. Unless you have an amazing portfolio, you need to have a reputable reference. Networking is key. Keep in touch with as many people as possible. People from school, people from a summer stock internship you may have had, and your professors, too. Also make sure your portfolio, as big or as small as it is, is the best representation of you and your work, and keep it neat, clean, and well organized. The presentation of the work is as important as the work itself.

Q: Why did you choose theatre over architectural lighting, or another form of lighting design?

A: Theatre is a collaborative art form. You can be a fine artist and paint in a room by yourself and that may turn you on, but the thing about doing theatre is that it is live. Sure, you can design a building and it's collaborative or you could design for a movie and it too is collaborative, but the big difference is that the end result for theatre is that it's live–there's an audience right there in the same room as the performers. There's a different kind of adrenaline rush that comes along with live theatre. I think, maybe we are all secretly adrenaline junkies! The designers, directors, and crewmembers who work on live shows like the Grammy's or the Academy Awards, must be serious adrenaline junkies because there's so much at stake; there's no margin for error on those productions.

    The other thing to remember is that it's "show business" not "show art," and as a business model, you have to diversify your skills. You have to start by assisting, probably as a draftsperson, or you might walk dogs, drive a taxi, usher, or become a guard at a museum to supplement your income. There is so much to do in New York that it makes it easy to be able to diversify. You learn to do architectural lighting and you also learn to use programs like Photoshop and After Effects. These are the skills that will also allow you to be hired by lots of different employers.

Q: Would you like the opportunity to share your knowledge and experiences by pursuing a career as a professor of lighting design one day?

A: I would love to teach one day–not only for the extra income, but the opportunity to work with and share my ideas with design students. But then, I've also had the thought, why would I want to teach when I tell people not to go into this field because it is so damned difficult? I feel like I'm constantly contradicting myself.

    I recently spoke with a good friend of mine who is an Emmy Award-winning set designer. He shared his perspective on this issue with me, since he recently took a teaching position at a local university. I asked him, "Why are we encouraging these kids to go into a

"The other thing to remember is that it's 'show business' not 'show art,' and as a business model, you have to diversify your skills."

Production photo, David Lander Studio
33 Variations, Eugene O'Neill Theatre, New York, NY
Directed by Moisés Kaufman
Lighting, David Lander
Costume, Janice Pytel
Set, Derek McLane

career that's so incredibly difficult? What percentage of them will actually stay in this field and have a successful career as a theatre designer?" His response was, "I don't approach it that way. I teach these students how to think, how to be creative, how to approach and analyze any give problem, to step outside of the box." What he teaches them can relate to life not just theatre. They are life skills. What he said really inspired me to think of theatre education in a much broader scope.

Q: Do you have any final advice you'd like to give young designers?

A: Yes. It is important to be unique and have your own voice. What gets you hired is your style, how you see things differently than others, and translate that idea onto the stage. Have a strong and distinctive point of view for each production, and always be true to yourself. Also, remember to have fun. If you are not having fun then it's not worth doing.

PETER NIGRINI –
PROJECTION DESIGNER
Friday, February 11, 2011

Peter Nigrini was born in Toronto, Canada but eventually found his way to the United States where, in 1993, he earned a degree from Dartmouth College. From there, he made the decision to enroll in Central St. Martin's College of Art and Design's International Scenography Centre (London), where in 1998 he received his M. A. under the program direction of Pamela Howard. When he returned to the United States, he began working in smaller venues in the Lower East Side and began to explore design, utilizing projection. Up until this point, Peter was a set and lighting designer, but he knew that in order to create an identity for himself in a city like New York, he needed an edge—and that edge was projection design.

His work has since been seen across the country as well as internationally, but Peter still calls New York his home. Although he continues to work in a number of design areas, he has recently created Broadway projection designs for Fela!, *and* 9 to 5: The Musical. *He has also designed* The Elaborate Entrance of Chad Deity, *by Kris Diaz, and* Wings, *by Arthur Kopit, for the Second Stage Theatre in New York City. He is a founding member, along with his Dartmouth classmates Kelly Copper and Pavol Liska, of the New York City experimental theatre company Nature Theatre of Oklahoma, where he has designed productions of* The Poetics: A Ballet Brut *and* No Dice, *which earned the group a 2007 Obie Award.*

Q: Can you tell me a little bit about the path you took to get where you are today?

A: Well, to go all the way back, I suppose some time while I was in high school, I realized that I might want to spend my life in the theatre, or at least thought that I did. I'm not sure how much you can really know about what you want to do with your life at that age. Both my parents were geologists, researchers, and they looked at me like they didn't know what the hell to do with me. I'm sure they were thinking, "What in the world is this all about?"

I then went to undergrad at Dartmouth on a science scholarship that I would lose should the good people of Westinghouse discover that I didn't want to become a scientist. I had to pretend for a little while that I was going to be a scientist both to placate my parents and to keep the scholarship. However, eventually I had to come clean and admit that I had no intention of becoming a scientist. So, at Dartmouth I studied and majored in theatre with a minor in film.

Looking back on it now, while I was at Dartmouth I probably ended up taking too many theatre courses. I was in the theatre department and also worked in the performing arts centre there, which functioned as a roadhouse as well as the college theatre. At the time, all of the touring shows were crewed by students. The full-time staff was quite small, not nearly big enough to crew a show, and the rest of the crew in the roadhouse was made up of students. Watching how that all worked was really a great view into what theatre was really like.

That was Dartmouth. I graduated and ended up doing some television in Los Angeles. I spent about two years working in television and decided I hated it; television wasn't for me. I then moved to New York and spent another three years working as an assistant designer while designing my own smaller shows.

Q: Were you a set or lighting designer?

A: At the time, I considered myself a scenic and lighting designer. The television work I was doing was either as an art director, assistant art director, or scenic charge. I spent a full season on a television show as the charge scenic artist before I had enough. After moving to New York, I was designing scenery, lighting, and on rare occasions, dabbling in projection.

At the time I hadn't quite really figured out that's what I wanted to do; I guess it was about five years after I'd been out of undergrad that I became increasingly interested in projection and video technology in the theatre. I also thought it might be a good time to go back to school, but I had no interest in doing that in the United States. Partly because I knew it would be a great opportunity to go somewhere else, and partly because I didn't feel like I was ready to sign up for three more years of school.

Having worked in Los Angeles and New York for five years, I felt like I had already learned a good part of what a graduate school in the United States might provide. Instead, I applied to a number of theatre programs in London. Eventually I enrolled in a program run by Central St. Martin's that was a one-year, twelve-month program. It was an incredibly intense, crazy program run by Pamela Howard. She had built a course of study at Central that was taught at Central St. Martin's in London and at the Hogeschool voor de Kunsten Utrecht. Students started in either one of these two places and spent their first three months in that particular location. The following three months were spent in one or two other cities somewhere in Europe. I, for instance, ended up going to DAMU, the national drama academy in Prague. It was fascinating because the faculty in each city taught something different; however, you didn't get to choose where you went; you were basically told where you would be going. There was one group of students who were sent to Seville to study street theatre, another that went to study film and media in Helsinki, and still others who were sent to Prague to study opera. Some people from London would end up going to Utrecht and some people from Utrecht would end up coming to London. You were basically shipped off to explore various performance styles.

The last six months of the program were spent working on your thesis, which happened either in London or Utrecht, but it didn't necessarily coincide with where you started. Pamela made those decisions for you; it was a little bit like joining the army. (Laughs). We were not only bouncing all over Europe, but also the students were from all over the world, bringing an even wider perspective to the group.

Q: Aside from being overseas, what made this program in London so different than a traditional MFA program in the United States?

A: What made this program unique was that we were studying "scenography" in Pamela Howard's view of the discipline. To be honest, they really didn't have much to say about lighting, it really was a program based primarily in the study of set and costume design with an emphasis on the relationship between designer and director. In the end, we were all basically working towards what might be called a directorial approach to design. Pamela's theory about scenography was that you have a scenographer and a director and they are, basically, co-equals serving as the creators of a production.

Having been taught in a way that forced me to think like a director was incredibly useful. Doing all of the dramaturgical work and textual analysis has had a great impact on my development as a designer. Whether the current system in the United States of how theatre is created is going to change to accommodate this, who knows? But, if nothing else, pedagogically, I think it was a useful provocation

"Having been taught in a way that forced me to think like a director was incredibly useful."

to make us think, to make us really take ownership of all of the ideas we were presenting.

In order to be accepted into Pamela's program, one of the requirements was that each candidate had to propose their thesis as part of the application process. In fact, that was the entire application. We also had to show some examples of our work, but that was about it. Everyone who was accepted into the program showed up with a thesis topic, and they ranged anywhere from a very conventional sort of theatre project to installation art to essentially what was a directing project.

The other aspect to our theses in addition to a written text was that they were all realized to a greater or lesser degree. I proposed an examination of the use of digital video in performance. In particular, it was a live performance using digital video or "V-Jaying" might be the best term for it, even though I'm not particularly fond of it. It involved an actor; another person who dealt with electronics in an audio capacity; and another person who dealt with electronics in a video capacity. I provided a text (written by Tim Griffen) and created a structure in which they would improvise in order to create a performance.

My favorite Pamela Howard story was that I think she actually hated my thesis, both in concept and realization. But, she accepted me. Maybe she thought she could cure me, I don't know. Perhaps that's why she made me study opera. She sent me off to design clothes for opera, in hopes of breaking my belief in projection.

A couple of days after I finished the program, I had also been working on a photo documentary project while I was in her course, of which she was aware. When we sat down to have coffee she said to me, "Well, I think maybe the best thing for you is to pursue this interest in photography." Basically, she was telling me not to be a designer. My response was, "Thanks for your advice." I have great respect for her and her opinion, and there are plenty of people who never would have said that to me. But, I look at it like this: if someone can be discouraged so easily, it's probably best they not do it, as it probably wouldn't have worked out anyway. I, on the other hand, knew it was what I wanted to do, and I believed I had to capacity to succeed.

Q: How much experience with video and digital work had you had prior to developing this project?

A: Well, some, but not much. I'd done a very low-fi projection project in New York prior that was all about 35mm slide projectors. It wasn't about video; it was about half a dozen 35mm slide projectors that had no automated system to run them. It was run literally straight from the Kodak Ektagraphic remote controls, screwed to a two by four in such a way that the projectors could be "performed." Also, while I was an undergraduate student there had been a big projection project that I had been the tech for, but that was very early on in my studies. Really, there wasn't a lot. What did help me quite a bit was that I was spending a lot of time, in an amateur way, as a photographer. I was also very comfortable with computers, but I wasn't a videographer. I had actually shot on film a bit, having been a film major, but I'd never plugged all these things together, and certainly not video.

The idea of actually using video as provided by computers in the theatre during the late 1990s was still very new. Theatres were still running video off of DVD players. Maybe there were data systems driving DVD players, maybe it was VHS or Beta tape or something like that, but it wasn't computers putting video on stage. Unlike now where every show we do has it content delivered by a media server of some kind. People certainly don't put DVD players in shows anymore. At that point, this was still relatively new, the idea that there could be real time playback and editing. It's not like I invented it—people were using it—but it was still in the world of the experimental.

Q: How did you decide to pursue a career as a projection designer then?

A: After spending a year in London, Prague, Utrecht, and various places, I thought about staying, but ended up returning to the United States. I also decided that saying I was a scenic, lighting, and projection designer was just ridiculous. It was just too much. So, I decided to pick two, and I chose lighting and projection. They seemed to cluster better and I basically started applying my worth that way. I discovered while there were maybe 600 lighting designers in New York there were only six projection designers. So, needless to say, me being number seven, as a projection designer seemed a smarter route than to be the 643rd lighting designer.

Q: Do you mean that there were only six or seven projection designers in the Union?

A: No, not in the Union. There were only six or seven projection designers in New York City. At that time, you could run down the list and get to the end of it at six. In retrospect, I don't suppose it was quite that accidental. It's by far the most fascinating design discipline as far as I'm concerned, so I'm very pleased that's the way it worked out for me, but some of it really had to do with access.

Q: When I was growing up and wanted to be a set designer, I had all of these predecessors I looked to for inspiration. Where did you look

for your inspiration since there really wasn't a lot of projection out there?

A: Right. You can sort of look to all of these big historical ones, Erwin Piscaor, Joseph Svoboda, and certainly, I mean, Batwin and Robin, Wendall Harrington, Jim Serling, their stuff existed out there at that time, but it hadn't coalesced into a real discipline yet. What continues to make this field so exciting is that at a relatively young age, I'm one of the people who gets to say, "This is the way we do things."

It's exciting; but it's also very challenging. When you are basically inventing it, the effort it takes to explain to people what it is we are attempting to create and how it is done is incredibly time consuming. I constantly find myself explaining to general managers, producers, and shops, "Well no, this is how we do this." It's because there's no established methodology. The entire structure of making theatre doesn't quite know what to do with us. Nine times out of ten we end up talking about where my tech table is going to be once the production moves into the theatre. That arrangement may seem petty, but it's actually really quite important. The way the communication happens between the director and other designers during that moment in that theatre is critical. If I'm over there in the corner, guess what? That's not going to work. I need to be relatively close to where the decisions are being made. So, there are upsides and downsides to how new this is.

Q: That's a great segue way to my next question. Where does the projection designer fit into this equation?

A: It really depends. I find that increasingly projection is not the afterthought that it often used to be. I think people have learned that it's best to start talking to a projection designer as early as possible. Sometimes the director walks in the door with a notion that there's projection in the show right from the start. That's one way it happens. I would say, maybe half of the shows I do, someone calls me and says, "Ok, we're doing this play and the director has an idea that involves projection." Another scenario I find is the result of set designers proposing an approach to a production that includes projection in some way, and develops this idea scenically until the point that the director and set designer agree on this approach and then decide to bring me into the conversation. And increasingly projection is actually written into the script. A lot of new plays are quite explicit about the use of projection; a number of playwrights are equally engaged in the idea that this is another narrative device of which they would like to take advantage.

Production photo, T. Charles Erickson
Fetch Clay, Make Man, Berlind Theatre, McCarter Theatre Center, Princeton, NJ, 2010
Directed by Des McAnuff
Lighting, Howell Binkley
Projection, Peter Nigrini
Costume, Paul Tazewell
Set, Riccardo Hernandez

    Then, obviously, there are the outliers. Sometimes, it's the lighting designer. On *9 to 5*, which I designed with Jules Fisher and Peggy Eisenhauer, it was really Peggy who suggested that the production would benefit from projection. She felt that lighting alone, or lighting as it's traditionally conceived, wouldn't be sufficient. A lot of what I was designing with them was crossing a bridge between light and projection. Jules and Peggy were looking at the set, this big office environment, and their concern was, and I think rightfully so, that light was going to be asked to transform the space in ways that might not be possible. It was a beautiful, but cold, mid-eighties office environment designed by Scott Pask that was an ideal starting point for the story being told. But as Peggy said, "I know that we're going to get into tech and then say, "Where's the "musical" going to come from?" And everyone's going to hope that lighting can sufficiently transform the environment. She was absolutely correct in saying that it needed more than that. It was really Jules and Peggy who pushed the idea of using projection. It is, however, rare for a lighting designer to be the first person to put the idea on the table.

Q: So, after the first draft of the set is done, you said that it's at this point when the other people may be brought in to join the team? Do you find you work more closely with either scenery or lighting?

A: I would say both at various stages of the process. Projection is just another component to the show and has various points of contact with all departments. It is in pre-production that working closely with the set designer is essential. On a technical level, we discuss the space I need for equipment and the surfaces on which we will be projecting; however, these are really secondary to the larger aesthetic questions. If the set designer and I are not composing stage pictures together, then we could be missing a wonderful opportunity to interject a more malleable compositional element to the stage picture that can offset, compliment, and complete the scenic environment.

I'm usually busy working with the set designer and director up until tech, and at the moment when the technical rehearsals begin, that's when my collaboration with the set designer wanes a bit and it's about the lighting designer and me collectively putting light on stage. Together it is the two of us, that is not to say that the lighting designer might not be an integral part of the earlier conversations, but certainly once in tech, this collaboration is essential.

It's also about the scale. In a large musical, where there is such a great deal of time and money being spent, a lighting designer can afford to be involved early on in the process, whereas for smaller productions, the unfortunate reality is that the lighting designer is most likely only really afforded the opportunity to be closely involved prior to technical rehearsals. As a result it is in the theatre that we can truly begin working through all of the specifics involved in combining lighting and projections.

Q: With the addition of the projection and video in so many productions, do you ask for more time to be built into an already tight tech schedule?

A: We certainly are considered when building the tech schedule, but do I succeed when I say that I need more time? Not so often. I think one thing that continues to be a big struggle for projection design is finding ways to move at the speed that is required. I do, however, think that we are all getting better at it. Speed really is the name of the game since there isn't any money being made during tech. The thought of expanding tech time is very rarely an option; we just need to work more efficiently. In reality, it's about more than just money; there are also the challenges of what is best for the production process, the performers, and other members of the creative team. If the process becomes too slow, I often find that the attention of the others in the room wanders, and the overall creative process deteriorates. In some way this need to work in the most efficient possible manner is really about respect. I would hope that I never have to ask a company to wait for my department; this of course is entirely unrealistic, but it is nonetheless a worthy goal.

I also think working with directors in an effort to help them understand what the proper process is for a projection designer is also very important. A lot of times, I'll sit down with them and explain my process. Whereas ideally, many times a director would like to get a particular moment to look absolutely right and then move on to the next look. More often than not, I try to encourage the notion that the tech process is actually going to be a sketching process where we can find a way to work more quickly and not spend time polishing each look. I believe our time is better spent in other ways so the finalizing of the cues could happen when we aren't tying up the entire design staff and performers. It may be a better use of time for everyone if we can present a sketch of where we're going to end up, see that the first time through in the technical rehearsal, and then sign off on what that is with the understanding of how the sketch will progress towards it's final form. For example, in some cases we can produce a still image and agree that in its finished form it should have movement. The time it will take to put the motion into the image is far beyond what anyone wants to wait or what the production can afford during a technical rehearsal. This same strategy can apply to a wide range of shortcuts that allow us to present the ideas and keep the production moving forward without either too great a time burden or hopefully, any negative impacts on the final work.

Sometimes, it's just about the technical concerns of the images. The resolution may be a little low or a bit rough, so we come back around and clean that up. So, it's a slightly different process in that way than it is for a costume designer or a set designer or especially a lighting designer. A great deal of what I do with my image editors and design assistants is figuring out how to get them to move as quickly as possible while explaining to the crews and the rest of the production team that, "Eventually, this is the way it's going to look."

I also find that being clear with the director about the time that it will take to fulfill various requests is very important. When they ask to see a particular idea, quite often I will say to them, "If we wait five minutes we can have a sketch, if we wait twenty minutes we can have a better sketch, and if we want to wait an hour you can have it finished. Which do you want?" I feel it is my job to be able to give them options. Each choice is legitimate in any given moment, but it's my job to be clear about these options and help a director understand what they are looking at in each case.

Top: Storyboard rendering, Peter Nigrini
Notes from the Underground, Yale Repertory, New Haven, CT, 2009
Directed by Robert Woodruff
Lighting, Mark Barton
Projection, Peter Nigrini
Costume, Moria Sine Clinton
Set, David Zinn
Bottom: Production photo, Mark Barton

Q: How do you illustrate your work prior to being in that discussion? With the set designer, he or she can usually convey exactly what the set will look like through an array of renderings and models. What do you share with the director?

A: Generally, I do very detailed renderings. I ask the set designer for a series of the model photographs representing every scenic state throughout the show. Then, I will either build static renderings from those model photographs or actually build video renderings of motion content into them. They are either built in a photo editor or a video compositing environment. After-Effects is my platform of choice. It is essentially Photoshop, but with time as a variable. It has a high learning curve, but once you understand it, it is a great tool.

For instance, I'll begin with the model photograph of Act One, Scene One, and identify and mask out all of the projection surfaces. Then, either in Photoshop (if I'm doing still images) or After-Effects (if I'm doing video), the projection content is composited into this masked model photo and, most importantly, further processed to simulate what the content will look like projected on the surfaces in question taking into account the surface materials, ambient light, perspective, etc. The biggest challenge in doing these renderings is being realistic about how it will ultimately look on stage. It can look great in the rendering, but in reality, how much light is really going to be bouncing off the set? How bright are the projectors? How much is the underlying surface going to affect the image, if I'm projecting on a concrete wall, how much of its texture is going to be visible? I'm always trying to accurately represent all those factors.

When I am rendering a show, it's all about being honest.

Through this process, I eventually end up with a moment-by-moment storyboard for the entire production. Increasingly, this part of the process is becoming more continuous with the building of the final materials–again looking for ways to be efficient. We will pull the set designer's model photographs into After-Effects, where we build the shows. We take the actual files or images of what we think we will be projecting and instead of out-putting them into a projection system, we composite them into a photograph of the model; in this way the storyboards are just another potential step in the process of building the final show. This also allows us to continue to refer back to them throughout the process, as they are often useful even once we have moved into the theatre.

I think all of the storyboarding is critical. If you're making it up in tech, you're in trouble–mainly because there's just not that much time. That isn't to say you always get it right either, because once you get in to tech, a lot of material gets thrown out. But, having done all of that work ahead of time provides you with the structural underpinnings of how to build the show. Even if you have to say, "This is completely wrong and I have to change it," at least the infrastructure is still there on which to make that change more efficiently. Of course, hopefully, most of the time you are right.

I would say this is actually the second or third step of the process of working with the director. I always like to start with a

Storyboard, Peter Nigrini
Camille, Bard Summerscape Festival, Annandale-on-Hudson, NY, 2006
Directed by Kate Whoriskey
Lighting, Jason Lyons
Projection, Peter Nigrini
Costumes, Ilona Somogyi
Set, Walt Spangler

much more general conversation about style and approach. I think everyone's instincts encourage us to become specific too quickly, and this often leads to shortchanging important early steps in the creative process. As a first step, I usually collect a wide range of images to talk about, "Does this image or series of images feel like what we think this feels like?" When design conversations begin with the question, what is it, rather than what does it feel like, then I know we are in trouble. Those kinds of questions are actually the most boring! "What does it feel like?" Now, that's an interesting question! I think the danger of projection is that it becomes illustration, and that is rarely good, as far as I'm concerned. If you're trying to communicate

"I think the danger of projection is that it becomes illustration, and that is rarely good, as far as I'm concerned."

information, I think it's much better to start in a much more abstract way. Sometimes the questions may not have anything to do with the show, but we may start off with language that is remote but visually relevant to the show. So, I think having to do with style, starting in an abstract way is very important.

I think that's what's exciting about the projection I tend to do. I like my work to be an integral component of the narrative, which is to say that without projection, the narrative just isn't there. It should be essential to the story, because if it's not, then it just becomes decoration and not theatrical. If it's not essential, it shouldn't be there. It's also our job as the projection designer to articulate just how essential projections are to the telling of the story. If they are not, it is equally our job to suggest that maybe the production would be better of without us. I think this is where the process of storyboarding is really critical in that it helps a director understand how all of the design elements can be integrated and how they can be relied upon as an integral part of the production. Without some sort of physical representation of this as a frame of reference in the rehearsal process, it is the rare director who will not simply work to fill those theatrical needs by some other means. Detailed storyboards make it possible to see where the director and other designers can rely on projections in similar ways we've come to rely on costumes, sound, lighting, and scenery.

For example, in designing *Fela!* the central plot point of the production is communicated entirely through projection. The entire play was about the fact that the government kills Fela Kuti's mother; that's the premise of the entire play. The farther we went in the process of developing the text, the more I realized the best way to communicate that information was through projection. We ended up with the climax of the production, the Storming of Fela's home, as a theatrical event made up almost entirely of projection.

It was imperative that I do enough development work to show the director and writer exactly how the projection could be integrated into the way the story was being told. If I couldn't do that, then they could never have confidence in the idea. Of course, they are expecting to have a script before we go into tech, and if I can't demonstrate to them what it is going to look like or what the impact of the projection will have on the scene, then it's completely reasonable that they are going to try and solve the problem in rehearsal their own way. That's why it is so very important to provide those projection ideas during the rehearsal process whenever possible. Not using a full system, of course, just some kind of visual that a director can use as a reference. A lot of times I will give them a copy of the script with a storyboard down the side, so as they are sitting in rehearsal they can see what we discussed and can be viewing it in the context of the rehearsal. Since most of the storytelling is being figured out in the rehearsal room, if you can't somehow demonstrate your ideas to them then, it will be too late by the time technical rehearsals roll around.

Q: Where do you find your assistants? I would think that would also be challenging.

A: Yes, it is incredibly challenging. I feel that I really have to cut my assistants from whole cloth, as they don't already exist. Of course, there are plenty of people who are interested, and I usually pull people in from editing or the film industry to work on the content side of what I do. Or, I'll pull in lighting designers to handle the system side, drafting, and lens selection. Of course, this tends to mean that there's always a whole category of knowledge that they are missing. So I do find myself teaching a lot, but I think that's my responsibility. None of my assistants want stay assistants; they are working with me to learn the craft.

On the rare occasion that I find a seasoned projection assistant, the work process is so diverse from designer to designer that the there's still a very steep learning curve to integrate a new person into my studio. As I result, I work very hard to keep the same people. I do think that projection designers are, slowly, moving toward a more common way of working. One of the main reasons why it's moving so slowly is because the systems we use for projection are so complex. From the edit environment through to the playback system and ultimately the display devices, it is a huge machine to understand. I assume schools are eventually going to come around and begin to integrate it into their training programs, but it's very, very expensive and always changing. In the end, the situation of projection design isn't that unique from sound ten years ago, and lighting thirty years ago, so I do think projection will settle in over time.

Q: If a young person were interested in pursuing projection design, what kind of advice would you give them?

A: I would find someone whose work you like and work with him or her. Frankly, I would say that to everyone who wants to be a designer. I'm not a big believer in graduate school. I know it can be the right thing for the right person, but it wasn't the right thing for me. Or, at least three years at Yale or NYU certainly wasn't the right thing for me. I can only speak from my own experience, but my decision was I think the right one for me, and I feel that these alternatives are often undervalued in the US.

I also think it depends on how much design experience you have, what sort of things you have done prior to graduate school, and on how much time you actually spent working in the theatre while getting your undergrad degree. I have some fundamental concerns about how the American system has institutionalized this type of education. In the past, you would have learned this as a journeyman. You would have spent your time working in the office of a designer, and you would have slowly gained the skills you needed and eventually, you would have reached the level where you could work on your own. I feel the things I've learned from making theatre are infinitely more valuable than what I learned sitting in a chair in a lecture, or even a laboratory environment in school.

Going back to my time at Dartmouth, I still feel that the most valuable things I learned were from working in the roadhouse. I wish, looking back, that I had spent less time in theatre classes and more time studying. There's far more interesting things to learn in college than just theatre. Don't get me wrong, I love theatre, but the best place to learn theatre is in the theatre, not in the classroom.

Another aspect to my decision not to go to grad school, to be perfectly blunt about it, was financial. I wasn't prepared to come out of graduate school in debt. I couldn't comprehend how you could start a life in theatre in debt. Because theatre isn't exactly a money making proposition. So, if you can't get through graduate school without taking out substantial loans, then I think it's a huge mistake. Once you're out of graduate school, there are going to be the years of scraping by, no matter what. The debt forces you into a set of choices that does not allow you the freedom you need in order to grow as an artist.

Q: You mentioned earlier that you felt like you had too many theatre courses in school. This is an interesting perspective, given that most courses don't encourage a lot of study in production. Is this why you seemed to think too much time was spent in the classroom and not in the theatre?

A: Yes. The theatre is where I think you learn theatre! Granted, I think in a graduate school environment, you are going to learn incredibly valuable things. You certainly need to learn from someone, and I suppose in an academic environment, that means going to class. But I also think there's a whole other model that doesn't involve going to class—one that involves finding someone to sit next to that can mentor you, teach you.

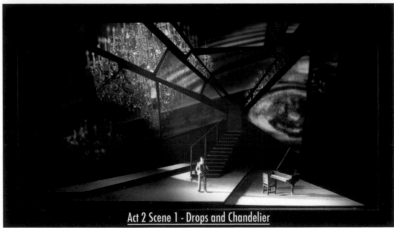

Top: Production photo, Peter Nigrini
Frau Margot, Fort Worth Opera, Fort Worth, TX, 2007
Directed by Frank Corsaro
Lighting, Matt Frey
Costume, Steven Bryant
Sets, Alison Nalder
Projection, Peter Nigrini
Bottom: Storyboard rendering, Peter Nigrini

I remember when I was studying to be a set designer that the ability to look at an eighteenth century wall elevation and understand what the moldings are and where all the details are and what that whole composition and proportions were, was really difficult to learn. It's ultimately about learning to see. I find there is a parallel issue with teaching projection designers. When I am working with my assistants, there are moments when I feel that I have provided them with a direction and I think that they can handle the execution of the design from that certain point forward, and I leave it their hands. Then I'll come back to it for review, and it's clear that everything we've covered has not really connected with them, that what I thought was a clear instruction was somehow not apparent to them. These visual ideas are still somewhat abstract and informational rather than visceral to them.

I ultimately think that's the real challenge in making the step from being an assistant to a theatrical designer. It's the ability to make sound, artistic decisions quickly and intuitively. Particularly for those of us who are lighting, set, sound, or projection designers, it's that moment-to-moment decision-making process and the ability to create on a tight schedule that is crucial to becoming a proficient designer. I think the process of seeing and responding to what you're seeing aesthetically is something you can really only learn by exercising those muscles. In my opinion, that can only happen by assisting and learning from experienced designers or by designing.

In one of my favorite, and perhaps apocryphal stories, a now established lighting designer got his start when he was an eighteen-year-old nobody, literally by walking in the stage door of a Broadway theatre and starting to look around. He told the house electrician that he just wanted to learn about what went on, and the house electrician first told him he wasn't supposed to be back there, but if the kid stuck by him, he would show him around and let him stay and watch the matinee. Remember, this kid had walked in off of the street. And it happened just like that. So, if someone emails me and asks me if they could come sit and watch or observe, my response is always, "No, you can't come sit and watch; but I'll put you to work on something." You're not going to learn anything from watching. Also, in the end, I think we are all just flattered that people are interested in what we're doing.

Q: Why do you think it is so difficult for young designers to find work in New York?

A: I think because there are so many more designers out there who are capable of performing at the highest level, that and producers now have more say than they used to. Now you sort of have a struggle between the producer's desires and the director's desires. It's sort of a form of horse-trading. For example, if the director isn't going to get his choice on the lighting designer because the producer has someone else in mind, then the producer may concede on the scenic designer, and so on and so forth.

I also think that there's a greater burden on designers, particularly of Broadway, because the financial implications for a designer failing are greater than they used to be. If a designer makes mistakes, or even just bad choices, the financial repercussions are much greater. There's more money at stake as the cost of producing rises and the timetables are such that there isn't time built into the schedule to correct problems, should they arise. This all leads to the desire for certainty when hiring designers for commercial theatre. Personally, I think this idea is bullshit, but when it comes down to it, the industry looks to designers who have successfully pulled off big shows, and they look for safety in that knowledge. A simple mistake could easily spiral into a million dollar loss. Any number of errors could affect the production schedule, which then might push backs previews or the opening date, and at that point, the cost implications could easily overwhelm a production. So, yes, the prospect of a million dollar mistake if it causes the production to fall behind schedule is not at all far fetched. The shows are highly technical, and they are enormously huge machines; however, I'm strictly referring to Broadway.

Q: Do you try to get work outside of the city (New York)? I ask this question because I often wonder how regional theatres can afford projection design.

A: Well, it's tough. I do work outside of the city, but projection is expensive. I think the conversations usually begin by me saying, "Give me all your money," and we go from there. It's so incredibly expensive that the assumption is that it cannot be afforded. For instance, the first number I'm going to give back is usually the entire budget for the show, and then we will try to scale it back from there. Because of that fact, I think it's very difficult for regional houses to use projection on a regular basis.

I do have the good fortune of having established some great relationships with supply houses and often will be able to make special arrangements to use equipment for out-of-town productions at a reduced rental cost. Ultimately, the rental houses want to establish relationships with working designers so they are more willing to work a deal for an out-of-town production in order to cultivate that relationship, even if it means the rental cost will be a bit lower than they might normally charge. That's the economics of the situation. It's possible, but it takes a good deal of finesse.

Q: It sounds like, apart from being a great designer, it's also important to be a good negotiator.

A: Negotiating is a part of what we do, and I think that's true of any designer. I certainly think that there are different approaches across the disciplines and between various designers, both in regards to the financial issues and the technical issues. I find that I, at a very minimum, need a clear technical understanding of how things are being done in order to do my work effectively. Maybe it's just my personality, but it's the way I work. Financially, it is to some degree the same. I work very hard to make the most of the resources available, and if I don't have a detailed understanding of how the cost of a design is arrived at, I can't ensure I am making efficient use of the resources. While this of course makes producers happy, it's also about allowing me to create the best possible design.

I feel that in the case of scenery, many of the budget choices are for the most part linear; whereas, the fine grain choices I'm making about projector types can have a huge financial impact on a show's budget, that may ultimately be way out of scale as compared to it's visual appearance. A lot of times, making the smaller projects work is about being able to negotiate with the shop and get equipment, for instance, at a cheaper rate on one show for four weeks because they know otherwise it's just going to sit in the warehouse unused anyway. Or, it's useful to be able to negotiate with them on using the older equipment when you can in order to save. Having that kind of flexibility, with the way the system is designed, allows a fair amount of "horse-trading" and makes a lot more shows possible. If I didn't do that, far less will be possible.

The interesting thing, and this is still an ongoing discussion among projection designers, is the way in which, to some degree, we run our own shops in addition to being designers. Who builds the actual show's content? We, or our assistants, do. I feel one of the big ongoing projects for all projection designers is both establishing it as a standard and explaining to producers that the fee I'm being paid is to design the show, not to build the show's content, and there's a huge difference between the two in both time and money. On top of that, there's also the need to rent the editing equipment. So, there's a rental component, there's the cost of materials, will the images be stock footage or archival footage or do we need to shoot the footage, these are the materials, or content costs. Then, there's the "construction" cost. There needs to be someone who takes the raw materials, such as the archival footage, or shot footage, and turns it into a finished product. That's a construction process, and it is not only very time consuming but costly as well. In many ways it parallels what sound designers are doing, but the way a sound designer will go about it is that they will say there's a composition fee, whereas I call it a construction cost.

Q: When, in your process, does system designs come into play?

A: Usually, as soon as the set is done. Of course there will have been conversations as the set is being designed about what is possible, but as soon as that is done, I will try to get the system design completed. The sooner I know the specifics of a system, the sooner all of the content development can begin in earnest. Knowing the details of the final system also allows the design process to flow much more naturally into actually construction phase. This is where the storyboard process comes into play. The idea is that by the time the storyboards are done, the show is half built. Also, if I want to fight for money, if the director or the set designer or the producers are saying, "This is our priority and if you need us to cut some scenery to pay for the projections then that's fine." That is a great opportunity; but if I haven't designed the system and can't really quantify it's cost before they start building the scenery, then the opportunity is lost. So, designing as soon as possible is critical.

Q: Do you feel any pressure to share your knowledge, or think of ways to offer resources to young designers who may be interested in this specific type of design work?

A: Absolutely. I don't feel pressure necessarily, but certainly an obligation. I've talked with lighting designers who teach at the college level, and we are in agreement that a format for teaching projection design should be developed. However, I think we are still one step away from passing it on, mainly because we are still trying to invent that process. For instance, with projection recently recognized in the Union, I feel a huge responsibility to get that right. Getting projection designers into the Union and making sure the contracts have been fairly compensated is something I've done a lot of work on. It's very important to me that all designers are treated as fairly as possible.

Generally speaking, here's how to think about it: you end up with a lot of people making a lot of personal sacrifices because we love theatre so much. In the end, that's not sustainable. It's a challenge I think we still face and it is especially true for my assistants. In the end, the amount of money assistants are paid is not enough on which to make a living. It may be enough to live on as a single, twenty-something, but it certainly is not enough for anyone who wants to build a career as an assistant and be financially independent or have a family. Yet, is that an appropriate role? If you think of all assistants becoming designers, then that's an acceptable transition, but if you think of assistants choosing to remain assistants as a career, like a Broadway associate, it's difficult to make enough money to live a complete life on that kind of income. I think it's important for all of us to come in to this knowing how to make a sustainable living doing this type of work.

Q: With as many young people graduating with a degree in theatre, what is it that you look for when hiring an assistant?

A: Ultimately, there's something beyond any of the skills that might be taught in a university. It's a certain quality that I look for in all of my assistants. It's a mixture of ambition and motivation that I look for. It also takes great leadership. I have a team of people who work with me, and I am but one in a team of people who work for this much larger entity, which is the production. Obviously, there are directors and producers involved, but there's also something very important about the person who can walk into that same room with an air of leadership and belonging.

Q: What final words of advice would you give to someone who is looking to find work as a projection designer in New York City, or for that matter, anywhere?

A: First and foremost, you need the financial freedom to be able to design for free. There were a number of shows I designed for little or no money both before I went to graduate school and after I finished graduate school. The money I was paid was certainly not enough to make a living, so I did temp work at a law firm in the middle of the night to pay my bills. What also helped quite a bit was that I found a rent-stabilized apartment. These choices afforded me the opportunity to do theatre for free with others who also didn't have any money. Now, some ten years later, we all make a pretty good living doing theatre, but back then, those were the sacrifices that had to be made, and I think they still have to be made as part of the process as a growing designer. Again, this comes to the question of debt. I didn't really have any leaving graduate school, and I think this was essential to my development as an artist and the development of my career.

   To be fair, in the end, it is a club, and getting into it is very hard. Is it difficult to design in New York? Yes, but only because there's so much competition. That's not to say you can't design anywhere else in the United States, because chances are much greater that you can.

   Also, if you have questions as to whether or not you should pursue a career as a designer, don't assist other designers in order to find your career, but assist as a way to learn how to be a good designer. I feel the way you get a career now, by today's standards, is by working with your peers and by creating an identity as a designer–become someone with whom others want to work. It used to be that you would assist someone who was, perhaps, your mentor, and eventually you would move up that ladder. Now, you work with people who are close in age and you all move up that ladder together.

If you don't start your career with the freedom to do shows for free, and do the kind of art you believe in, and work with your peers who are also in the same circumstance, then you aren't ever going to rise up to the top of whatever ladder you want to climb. If you are only an assistant, then you will be an assistant for life. Don't get me wrong, there are great assistants out there, career associates who don't want to be designers, who are brilliant and who make good money. But, to be a great designer, you need to do both: assist and design. You should assist instead of, or in addition to graduate school, but you also need to be doing your own work. It is these two things that will lead to relationships with directors and other designers and will become your cohort, your colleagues.

KENNETH POSNER – LIGHTING DESIGNER
Monday, March 14, 2011

Kenneth Posner is one of the busiest lighting designers working on Broadway. Between 1988 and 2011, Mr. Posner has designed over forty shows on Broadway and well over fifty shows off-Broadway. His designs range from the reality of Mrs. Warren's Profession *to the stylized, camp presentation of the off-Broadway hit* The Toxic Avenger. *Whether it's a show that requires a restrained and delicate hand when cuing or one that calls for an explosion of pattern and intense color, it seems Mr. Posner's work runs the gamut of what is both dramatically appropriate and theatrically exciting.*

In 1991, Kenneth was nominated for a Drama Desk Award for Machinal, *and his most recent accolade is a Tony Nomination for* The Merchant of Venice, *which starred Al Pacino. He also received a Tony Award for* Coast of Utopia: Shipwreck.

I was asked to meet Mr. Posner at the Neil Simon Theatre, and immediately upon entering the lobby I realized that I was meeting him at a very busy time in the production process. He had just wrapped up a rehearsal where he was fine-tuning his lighting cues for an upcoming production. He had a small window of opportunity to meet with me before returning to the theatre for a preview performance of the new musical Catch Me If You Can.

Q: Do you remember when you were first introduced to the theatre world?

A: My first exposure to the theatre was when I was six years old, when I started doing community theatre. My mother was involved in it, so that's how I was introduced to the theatre; that's where my passion for the theatre was born. Ultimately, I think that's what drives all of us as artists and as designers–passion. I kept with it, starting when I was about 15 years old, by doing summer stock. Since I grew up here, I was immersed in this world from a very young age.

When I was in high school, I was working at the New York Theatre Company on East 90th Street doing off-Broadway shows working as a carpenter and an electrician, or whatever I could do that got my hands dirty. I just wanted to be immersed in the theatre world. I was exposed to a lot of theatre as a young boy, and I understood the urban aspect, so the big city wasn't an intimidating factor at all; in fact, I really embraced it.

To be honest, summer stock was the foundation for my entire career. What I learned by doing all of those years of summer stock was the importance of developing great people skills, the ability to work quickly, and the true meaning of collaboration. It was there where I learned about blending different ideas from a wide range of people and influences.

Q: Where did you go to college for your training?

A: I began my training at Boston University, where I was accepted into their undergraduate design program. After I had been in the program for a while, I realized it really wasn't the place for me. I realized that I really wanted to be a designer, and at that time, the faculty at Boston University didn't think that I had the necessary skill sets or the vision to be successful. So, after my second year there, I went to work at the Berkshire Theatre Festival. While I was there, I met one of my mentors, Jeff Davis, who happens to be a wonderful lighting designer. I also met David Potts, who was the resident set designer for the Festival at the time. They both strongly encouraged me to not abandon my education if I was really serious about becoming a designer. At that time, David was also on faculty at SUNY Purchase, and it was through developing those two relationships during the Berkshire Theatre Festival that I was able to segue right from Boston University, which was not a positive experience, to SUNY Purchase, which was truly an amazing experience. Meeting those two gentlemen was one of the best things that ever happened in my life and certainly in my career. To have them embrace me and help guide me in the right direction was critical to my development as a designer. So, as far as lucky breaks in this industry, that was probably the first, luckiest thing that ever happened to me. There have been many lucky breaks in my life along the way, but that was definitely "lucky break" number one.

I went on to finish my studies at SUNY Purchase, where I was fortunate to have Billy Mintzer, who is no longer with us, as my primary lighting professor and mentor. I was also able to study under Brian MacDevitt, who came to SUNY Purchase to teach at the same time.

"To be honest, summer stock was the foundation for my entire career."

Q: What was so special about the training you received at SUNY Purchase that you believe gave you an edge?

A: I believe, along with learning about lighting design, I learned how to think like a director. I also learned about the relationship between a lighting designer and a director. I learned how to be a storyteller and I really learned how to analyze a script. We spent a lot of time discussing what the plays were about and how that information is transferred into a visual idea, how you take that visual idea and weave it into a lighting idea. And finally, how you take that lighting idea and put that on the stage. More than almost anything else, it was an immersive education about the philosophy of light. However, that doesn't mean there wasn't a solid practical application because there was. I just remember learning how to think and respond emotionally about a piece.

I continued to do summer stocks for the rest of my college career, which led to, what I guess I am calling my "lucky break" number two. I was hired to be the resident lighting designer in the second stage at the Berkshire Theatre Festival (where I worked with David Gallo), while also serving as Jeff Davis's assistant for his main stage designs. I actually spent nine seasons at the Berkshire Theatre Festival, where I graduated from being the resident designer on the second stage to becoming the resident designer on the main stage. Eventually, I scaled back from only designing for the main stage to only doing a couple of shows a season. After nine seasons at the Festival, I finally passed that torch onto someone new; it was time for me to move on.

I can't stress enough how important those summer stock years were to me and to the development of my professional career here in New York. I met a lot of great people, including Michael Greif who went on to direct *Rent*. He is probably the collaborator with whom I've had the longest tenure in the business. I also met and became friends with Gordon Edelstein, who is now the artistic director at the Long Wharf Theatre. When I was at the Berkshire, he was their artistic director. It was those early relationships and early contacts that really helped me build a solid foundation for my eventual New York design career.

Q: Was the transition from Summer Stock work to New York professional theatre difficult?

A: I was able to segue from that summer stock experience into the New York off-Broadway and off-off-Broadway world quite successfully. It was very early in my career when I came to New York and got a job at the New York Theatre Workshop. R. J. Cutler, who was also one of the directors I worked with on the second stage at the Berkshire Theatre Festival, came to New York around 1988 to direct a show off-Broadway. I remember it was my first professional design job in New York City; it was a design for the Australian play *Emerald City*. Jim Youmans was the set designer, who happened to be a friend and colleague of mine from when we were at SUNY Purchase as classmates. I guess that experience was the third luckiest thing that happened to me.

Q: Did you work as an assistant designer while you were designing shows?

A: Yes, while I was designing smaller shows of my own, I was also assisting for about five years. I would design smaller off-Broadway shows and pay the bills and buy groceries with the assistant design work. It worked out quite well for me.

Q: What are some of the challenges young designers will face when trying to get design work in the city?

A: I think there are a number of issues; I think there has been an evolution of the nature of this business. Quite frankly, New York City isn't adding new theatres every year; in fact, we are losing theatres, which means there are less and less venues available for young designers to find work. And the older generation of designers, me included, will continue to work in small spaces. We will work off-off-Broadway, with the right director, because of the relationships we've built over the years, and I think that makes it very tough for the next generation of designers who are looking for their first design here in the city.

Q: Did you choose to become a theatrical lighting designer over working, for example, in the architectural lighting industry or for industrials?

A: I don't know if I chose it or if I just fell into it. What I love about the theatre is that my passion is the theatre. My medium, my inlet into the theatre just happens to be light, but I love the storytelling aspect of what we do in the theatre. I've done a little architectural lighting and I've also done some industrials and corporate work, but I'm really not that good at it. Honestly, I don't enjoy it that much, either. There are much better designers out there who can do a great job with those types of events, so I follow my own rule when it comes to those kinds of jobs: stick with what you know. Obviously, I've done opera and some dance because there is a storytelling aspect inherent in those forms as well.

Production photo, Derek McLane Studio
Little Women, Virginia Theatre, New York, NY, 2005
Directed by Susan H. Schulman
Lighting, Kenneth Posner
Costumes, Catherine Zuber
Sets, Derek McLane

Q: When you are hired to work on a project, do you ever have an opportunity to suggest other designers with whom you would like to work on the project?

A: It doesn't work that way for lighting designers. In this industry, it really is the director and the set designer who are the first two on board for most productions. Lighting designers get their work from the director and the set designer. Occasionally, a producer might throw my name out there, but it is only with the director's blessing that you get to do the project.

Q: Was there a defining moment in your early career where you made a conscious choice to live the life of a freelance designer as opposed to a more stable career?

A: I'm not sure I can necessarily pinpoint one defining moment, but freelancing was always my philosophy. I'm a lighting designer. I'm always going to be a lighting designer, and this is the life that I have chosen. Which means, I'm always going to be working from job to job without the knowledge or security of where or what my next project will be. I made that choice as far back as when I transferred to SUNY Purchase–it was just what I knew I wanted to do. I wanted nothing more than to be a lighting designer.

Q: Since you also have a successful career in the regional theatre community, what do you find to be the greatest differences between working regionally and working on Broadway?

A: Well to start, they are two really different animals. In regional theatre, it is community-based theatre so it's tied into its own artistic vision, and it is really nice to be welcomed into and create within that community of artists. You're also dealing with people who are doing up to twelve shows a season so you really are a guest in their environment. Also, the expectation of the work is based completely on the artistic vision you bring to them as opposed to commercial theatre, which is based on the fact that they need the show to be hugely successful so it can make a profit. In commercial theatre, the work isn't being done so people can get closer to God; it's being done to make money. Occasionally both can occur simultaneously and that's really what makes what we do very special.

Q: Does working in regional theatre, as opposed to commercial theatre, affect your design choices?

A: It certainly can, but it really affects the process more than anything. I guess the collaborative part of both regional and commercial theatre is very similar, because in both situations you've sat down and read the play and talked about the idea and have come up with a visual language. The show then gets designed, and you've collaborated with the theatre and their schedule as well as had discussions in regards to timing and budgets. In my experience, it's in the budgets where things are different in regional theatres since the budget limitations are much more severe than they are in the commercial industry. Even though the entire scenario I just laid out holds true in commercial theatre, in the end, you answer to both the artistic vision as well as the business vision. Commercial theatre is a combination of balancing the artistry of what we do along with the business aspect, which is just as important.

Ultimately, it's about asking the question, "Is this a $130 or $140 experience?" And what I mean is that the show not only needs to be a visually exciting experience, it also needs to deliver on an overall storytelling, visceral, experience. You don't necessarily have to answer that question in the same way when you work in the not-for-profit regional theatre setting. Because of that, you can take a much higher artistic risk in regional theatre than you can in commercial theatre.

Q: There's also a collaborative component to working in the theatre, meaning, we work together with others instead of in a studio, alone, creating our art. Does that social component energize you as a designer?

A: That may be true, but for me, it really is the social aspect woven into the artistic aspect that I am drawn to. It's the ability to take different points of views, different ideas, and different ways of doing things to create an integrated theatre experience that's really exciting for me.

Q: When it comes to formulating your design idea, is your process different for each type of theatrical experience?

A: Not really, because it ultimately comes down to one thing—the story you are telling and how you want to tell it. Therefore, I think the design approach is identical. Obviously, the results of the designs are much different, but the approach is almost exactly the same. *Mrs. Warren's Profession*, for example, takes place in four locations over the course of about a week, and it's certainly a naturalistic play, but it still has an arc to it. So, for that play as opposed to *Catch Me If You Can,* the lighting vocabulary is going to of course be different. It will have a much more naturalistic quality to the light that will still be theatrical, but we need to convey to the audience that we are in real places. As a lighting designer in musical theatre, you are given permission to explode and go into fantasy world, which is, ultimately, the biggest difference between designing a musical and a straight play.

Q: How does having a show like *Wicked* impact your decision to accept or reject designs? Are you able to be more selective?

A: Well, first of all, I am very lucky to have designed *Wicked*. Only a small percentage of designers are fortunate enough to have that happen in their lifetime and it definitely gives you some financial security. It also gives you the ability to pick and choose projects more selectively. I know that if I didn't have that show, I would not be able to be as selective as I am. Secondly, I also know that I would not be able to commit as much time to each project as I currently do. So, as an artist, it's a true luxury to be able to concentrate on one project and give it my full attention.

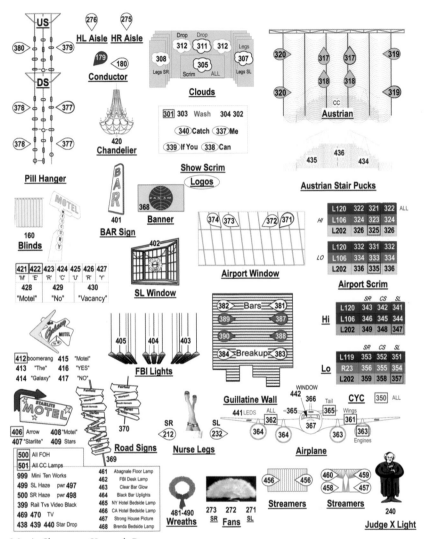

Magic Sheet – 1, Kenneth Posner
Catch Me If You Can, Neil Simon Theatre, New York, NY, 2011

Q: Are you up to speed with all of the new software and technology that is out there for lighting designers?

A: I didn't really get all the digital training and frankly, I'm really pretty inept at it. I tend to surround myself with people who are fluent and comfortable with it, and I have them teach me as much as they can. What is so wonderful is I can say to them, "Here's an idea I have.

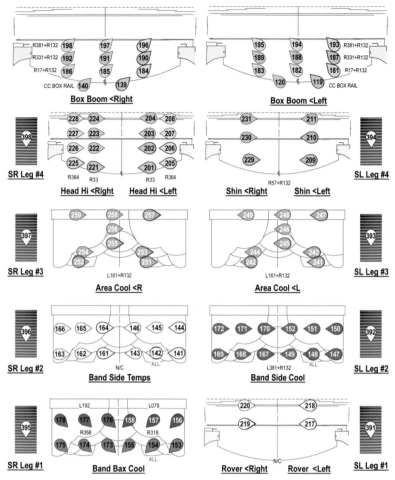

Magic Sheet – 2, Kenneth Posner
Catch Me If You Can, Neil Simon Theatre, New York, NY, 2011

Translate it. Interpret it." And they are able to do it. I am actually at a great disadvantage when it comes to technology; however, I never really felt like it was a great drawback to my career because early on I knew enough of that technology to get by. However, it's just exploded so quickly over the last few years that I'm simply not as competent as my assistants are, so I really do rely on their talents and skills in those areas.

Q: When you are faced with projections as part of the design language, how does that affect your work as the lighting designer?

A: Having no control over the brightest lighting source on stage can often times become problematic for me, whether it is a projector, a series of projectors, or an LED screen. I certainly hold projection designers in very high regard.

As far as design goes, I really learned from Wendall Harrington, who is probably one of the most brilliant storytellers I've ever met in my life. I admire her not just in her media projection, but also as a human being. I've learned so much from just listening to her analyze a script and attaching an idea to it. Her understanding of timing and musicality of an idea is just incredibly versatile in that regard. So, I definitely admire the artistry that projection can bring to a production; however, that being said, I haven't personally enjoyed the experience where projection was used to enhance the storytelling. I have seen projects where I thought it was used more effectively than others, but I'm just not crazy about big projection screens on stage. I think it is getting better and better, and I think it will continue to, but right now I find that it can really overpower the story that's being told. It can especially overpower the ability for an audience member to focus on an actor and the story that they are telling, and to follow the text. I do think when it is done well, those problems are minimized, but they don't go away completely.

Q: Do you remember having to hire your first assistant, and if so, how did you know what to look for or how to go about hiring someone to work with you?

A: I've always had at least one person assisting me on projects, and that pool of people expands and contracts depending on how busy I am. I recognize that certain people have really great skill sets in one area but perhaps not in another, so I try to surround myself with people who are right for the projects I happen to be working on. I try to choose the right kind of passion, spark, and competency in an assistant for each specific project.

Q: How many assistants do you employ at your studio?

A: It varies depending on my workload. The studio experience for me is a very private one. I lay out the entire show, or I lay out enough of the ideas that I can give it to a very experienced associate who's worked with me for many years to take the ideas and expand them into a working light plot. I like for my associates to come to the design meetings. I try to have them come to as many of the large group collaboration, storyboarding sessions, so they're fully informed about the direction we are taking on a particular project. This way, they really understand what they are drafting, why they are drafting it, and what the idea is. They're also at the meetings so they can catch my mistakes and suggest their own ideas for me to consider. I love that part of the collaboration. I try to keep my core of assistants and associates very small–I don't really like to expand unless I absolutely have to. I have my comfort zone that I try to stay within. I also do not have a separate studio, so I work from home. It makes it easier for me that way. However, working from home occasionally has its disadvantages, but for the most part, I get to be near my family more, which is very important to me.

Q: When you are in tech or previews for a new production, how do you handle suggestions from people outside of the immediate design team, like a producer, for example?

A: He who pays the piper calls the tune so, in that regard, a producer gets a large share of the votes. Usually, really experienced and great producers will give their notes to the director instead of coming to me directly. That's really the difference between a great producer and one who is not! It's not to say I don't have a relationship with the producers who might casually say, "What's going on here, Ken? What's your thought with this look? Is it going to be like that? I'm concerned about this." That type of thing I am fine with. I appreciate that they trust me and are comfortable enough to come to me with those concerns, but when it comes to really big ideas, they all get filtered through the director. It's not a democracy–it can't be. If it were, it would be chaos. There has to be one vision, and that's the director's vision. And, until someone decides it's not going to be that person, that's who you listen to.

Q: Working as a Broadway designer seems to demand that you be multi-faceted in your understanding of not only the art of lighting design, but all of the business aspects that go along with working in the commercial theatre as well.

A: It's so true. When you are a lighting designer in commercial theatre you also function as sort of a co-producer, which is a huge part of being a designer. You have to think like a director. You have to think like a designer, and you have to think like a producer for the overall

success of the show both artistically and financially. You have that
responsibility; I actually like that aspect of commercial theatre.

**Q: There seems to be a great deal of mystery about how a designer
gets their first Broadway show. How did you land your first Broadway show?**

A: My commercial theatre career was born out of regional theatre,
which is where about fifty percent of commercial theatre shows
start; in regional theatres. My first commercial show was called
Getting Away with Murder that Jack O'Brian directed. It started
at the Old Globe Theatre in San Diego, and Jack O'Brian hired me
to do two plays that season. One was an A.R. Gurney play and the
other was *Getting Away with Murder* by Stephen Sondheim, which
meant that I was doing two back-to-back plays at his regional theatre. It just turned out that *Getting Away with Murder* was transferred to New York, so that's how I found myself on Broadway. I
snuck on by way of a regional theatre job. I actually think that's
true of most designers; you sneak onto Broadway. You have to. I
did *Getting Away with Murder,* and then I did a couple of shows
at the Roundabout. All of a sudden, the play I designed at the
Roundabout moved to the Golden. It was called *Sideman,* which
was directed by Michael Mayer during the mid-1990s. Again, I
was designing in the regional theatres and then the shows were
being transferred to Broadway. So, all of a sudden, I've done a few
Broadway plays.

Another example was the play *The Last Night of Ballyhoo,*
which started at the Alliance Theatre in Atlanta during the Olym-
pics. The show was in the second space, which was located in the
basement. That space is a very small, intimate little theatre with
probably a hundred and ninety-nine seats. From there, it moved to
the Helen Hayes Theatre on Broadway. So, all of a sudden, I've had
six shows on Broadway, and I'm this new guy doing the lights. Now,
people are noticing my work and saying, "Where'd he come from?"

Even though many of these shows started in regional theatre
venues with the hope that they could transfer to Broadway, there was
certainly no guarantee. Also, there's no guarantee that I would go
with the show. There was, and remains, no contractual obligation to
take the original artistic staff to Broadway. In my case, it was simply
that the producers seemed to be happy with the way things looked
and the way I was managing the show. Therefore, they wanted me to
continue on with the project.

Q: *The Coast of Utopia* **was a fascinating project where three different lighting designers were used; one for each part of the trilogy. Was
that a unique design situation for you?**

A: Well, Brian MacDevitt and I are really close friends. We have
known each other for twenty-five years and have taken very similar
career paths. I've also known Natasha Katz quite a while, as well.
In fact, she was someone I assisted when I first got out of school.
It really came down to the three of us all having a relationship
with Jack O'Brian, the director, and him being comfortable with
the idea of working with all three of us. Looking back on it now,
I think it was a great opportunity for Jack to work with three different lighting designers who all approached the work in their own
unique way. Even though the set design and the costume design
were of one hand, by injecting three different lighting designers
into that process, Jack was able to expand and really explore the
work in a fresh way for each of the three plays.

**Q: Having "people skills" seem to be critical in this industry. Can you
talk a bit about interpersonal skills and their importance?**

A: That is very true. I've noticed, recently, that there is a sense of
entitlement with many of the new generation of designers. There
seems to be this notion that, since they have their Master's degree and
they've got the skill sets, they should be offered a Broadway show or a
regional theatre design. The reality is, that this isn't how this business
works, and the answer to how it works is really quite simple. The one
thing this new generation of designers is missing is life experience and
theatre experience. Theatre is probably the last occupation left in the
world, except possibly for medicine, where you have to go and appren-
tice or intern with someone in order to gain the necessary real world
experiences to be able to function in this industry. Getting a college degree is wonderful, but it is only the first of many steps a young designer
must take in order to really be ready to design at this level. The fact
is, you can only learn that on the job–that's life experience. That's not
something you learn at college, nor should you.

**Q: Why do you think the majority of the current generation of young
designers doesn't embrace the idea of interning?**

A: It's primarily because it's not necessarily the career path of many
of their peers, so they don't understand how our industry really
works. They see their peers, who are pursuing a degree in business
or marketing, for example, and those students are told that once

Production photo, Paul Kolnik Studio
The Coast of Utopia [Part 2 – Shipwreck], Vivian Beaumont Theatre, New York, NY, 2006
Directed by Jack O'Brien
Lighting, Kenneth Posner
Costumes, Catherine Zuber
Sets, Bob Crowley and Scott Pask

they have their degree, they will be earning $50,000 a year and then after four years they will be earning six figures. Here in the theatre, that just isn't our reality.

Q: What is it that you like the most about being a lighting designer?

A: It's definitely the collaboration. Enjoying success with a group of colleagues is wonderfully gratifying. Even when the work was considered a failure, knowing that you just have to come back and fight harder the next time. Play to win. But if you lose, pick yourself up and try again.

Q: What do you dislike the most about this profession?

A: I really try to stay as positive as I can, but if I had to choose one thing, I guess what I dislike the most is that the theatre sometimes pulls me away from my family more than I want. My family is extremely supportive, and for that I am very lucky. They are great, but I feel like, because we work so many hours, it's challenging. Having a personal life as well as a successful professional life is very, very demanding. You do find ways to work around it, though. For me, I don't accept every project I am offered; I try to be more selective because of the needs of my family.

Q: SUNY Purchase seems like it is a very strong, conservatory type program. Do you recommend that kind of an education when you are asked for advice on choosing a training program?

A: I would not recommend that kind of a program at all. When people ask me about college, I always urge them to go to a really, really great liberal arts school. You can certainly pursue theatre while you are there, there's no reason not to, whether it's through course work or extracurricular involvement. It's important to get a well-rounded education, and then balance that education by working as many summer stocks as you can. Then, if you are really passionate about it, go and find someone you admire and try to work with them as an intern and then, hopefully, as an assistant. Or, go on to graduate school to hone your craft. I've seen too many people in their junior and senior years of college who, all of a sudden, discover that they really do not want to do this anymore. And you know what, at eighteen or nineteen years old, you shouldn't have to know what you are going to do for the rest of your life. You should be allowed to change your mind; that's a good thing. Finish your degree, get that piece of paper and then you can go pursue whatever it is you want to pursue. That's really why I urge people to get a well-rounded education, because it just gives you more flexibility in your junior and senior years of your undergraduate degree.

Having said all of that, I would not change a thing about what I did. I made it work for me, but it's not the advice I would give to someone today. I guess what I'm saying is, "Don't do what I did; do what I say." There are some people who are so focused and driven that they may not take your advice, and that's fine, too. At least you have made them think about it. Personally, I know there is nothing I can do other than theatre. When I'm not doing theatre, I'm not very happy.

Q: What three books do you think every designer needs to have on his or her shelf?

A: Rather than three individual books I would actually say read as much as you possibly can about the craft and the art of lighting design from any and all sources. I'm sure you've heard this already, but *The Magic of Light* by Jean Rosenthal would be mandatory reading for all prospective lighting designers. I would also suggest that you read, as well as explore, art—especially paintings. In this industry, it is critical to have a solid understanding about the emotional qualities of Impressionism or Surrealism or Naturalism. Really understanding art and art history as well as architecture—that's what I would recommend for all theatre designers.

Q: What final words of advice would you share with young designers about training and entering the field of professional design?

A: I really try to stress to the next generation of designers that they need to balance their academic and educational experiences with professional education and experiences early on in their career. It's as simple as getting them to understand how critical it is to go and do summer stock theatre. First of all, it teaches you how to get a job. For as many summer stock jobs I was hired, I was probably rejected by at least ten others. You understand how to face rejection; you also understand competition. I'm forty-six years old and I still don't get hired for certain jobs that I really want to design, and that's OK. Ultimately, I want to be involved in shows where I am wanted.

Whenever a young person who is interested in theatre asks for my advice, my first question for them is always, "What are you doing this summer?" Because, really, if you are able to work in an environment where you are mounting four shows in six weeks or ten shows in ten weeks, that's where a young designer really hones their skills. Developing the ability to work quickly, solve problems quickly, and collaborate quickly are still the best ways to cut your teeth in this industry.

"Really understanding art and art history as well as architecture—that's what I would recommend for all theatre designers."

Afterword

Quite often, an idea is just an idea and a dream is just a dream. However, in the case of this particular project, an idea that was only a dream back in 2008 quickly became my reality in 2010. I was going to embark on a journey that was about as far from my comfort zone as humanly possible.

The project began with what I thought was a fairly innocuous statement I made during a faculty meeting in the fall of 2008. When the chair of my department asked what I was planning on accomplishing during my upcoming sabbatical, I blurted out, "I'm going to write a book." As soon as I spoke those six words, I quickly checked to see if they were within arm's reach, still floating in the air between us; with any luck, I could quickly gather them up and stuff them back into my mouth before anyone heard me. Sadly, that was not the case. At that moment most of my colleagues, including the chair of my department, glanced up and without hesitation said, "OK. Great." And just like that, I had committed myself to writing a book.

Having stated my intentions, I knew what I wanted the book to be, but going about it was another thing altogether. It had been close to twenty years since Arnold Aronson's book, *American Set Design I* had been published. Aronson's book was the gold standard by which other books were measured when it came to getting a glimpse into the lives of working designers. Since 1989, the theatrical designers of the American theatre landscape had changed dramatically. Most of the designers in current Playbills were not those who had been featured in Mr. Aronson's book, and I saw a void that needed to be filled. I'd often wondered why a new book had not yet been written. Why wasn't anyone interviewing the designers who were currently working in New York theatres? I would soon discover the answer.

I digress. I've been a designer and an academician my entire career, and the thought of writing a book was akin to the thought of performing open-heart surgery; I possessed neither the experience nor the ability to do either.

Or so I thought. I quickly learned that the moment I said the words, "I'm going to write a book" out loud, that simple phrase began to take on a life of its own. I was reminded of something one of my colleagues once said to our MFA candidates: "Courageously stating your goals and dreams aloud—ideally and with exquisite detail—makes them part of your future reality." This phrase would prove true in many different ways and on a number of occasions as the process of creating this book began to unfold.

I'd elected to take a one-semester sabbatical to complete the bulk of the manuscript. Giving myself just under six months in which to write, I knew I had my work cut out for me. Not only had I never written a book before, I also hadn't met any of the designers I wanted to interview, nor did I have a personal or professional connection to any of them. I was also informed that it could take years and, in some cases, an entire career to write a book. And don't forget trying to find a publisher. That, too, could take a lifetime. The more I thought about the reality of this task, the more terrified I became. Despite my concerns, I continued to press on.

I have to admit, anxiety is a strange and powerful emotion. As soon as I decided to write this book, I immediately began to question whether my "A" list of Broadway designers would even want to participate. I'm someone who enjoys order and consistency, so I found myself already concocting roadblocks and pitfalls long before I even tried to contact the designers. Consequently, I talked myself out of my original proposal to focus on Broadway designers, and decided that it might be more "realistic" to interview designers I knew. I would ask colleagues who were regional theatre resident designers, college professors who designed in the academic field, and designers who spent their careers freelancing. This was safe. This was something I was comfortable with. This, I thought, I could handle. As soon as I changed course and decided to take this "safe" path, my passion for the project diminished. I was no longer excited. I felt, essentially, like I was letting myself down. I had compromised my goals before I had even begun. While I have tremendous respect for my colleagues in this profession, writing about the careers of my peers just wasn't what I truly wanted to do.

I was, however, *truly* excited by the opportunity to interview the designers who had served as inspiration to my work over the past ten to fifteen years. I had been following the careers of many of the designers who are featured in this book for quite some time. I thought it was vitally important that the current generation of designers studying theatre have a chance to hear how designers in this new millennium found their "path," but I didn't think there was a chance in hell that they would have any desire to meet with me, a virtually unknown designer and educator from the state of Arkansas who happened to be writing his first book. Thankfully, my attitude was about to change. With the encouragement of my dear friend Tim Saternow, I was reminded that I shouldn't compromise my original goals. He insisted that I set the bar as high as I wanted and extend invitations to each and every designer I believed had a story to tell. He also reminded me of one very important fact: Every designer, regardless of his or her successes, wants to be heard. Although still somewhat skeptical, I pulled out my list of twelve current Broadway designers with the hope of securing interviews with at least six. I sent each designer an email, and less than thirty days later, ten out of the twelve had agreed to participate. And just like that, the book was becoming a reality.

Each interview was incredibly inspiring, but it was during my conversation with Christine Jones that another opportunity was born. As our interview was coming to a close, I casually mentioned that I really wanted my foreword to be written by a director who had worked with some of the designers I was interviewing. Christine then asked, "Who did you have in mind?" Mustering all the courage I had, I said, "I was really hoping to ask Michael Mayer to write it, but I don't know him." She quickly responded, "Oh, he would be great! Let me call him for you and see when he is available to meet with you." Before I knew it, she had handed me her phone and, in a matter of seconds, I was having a conversation with Michael Mayer. Two months later, I was sitting in Michael's kitchen, eating a piece of cake and discussing my book as well as the current state of the American theatre world. We talked as if we had known each other for years. As I left the interview I thanked Christine and ended the interview by saying, "If you ever need a Union design assistant, give me a call. I'd love to work with you." Little did I know what that simple sentence would mean to me in the months to come.

By early May 2011, I had completed all of my interviews and began the process of transcribing over 100,000 words into a manuscript. At this point, I still didn't have a publisher and had been rejected by well over thirty publishing houses. Was I getting discouraged? A bit. Was I going to give up? Not a chance. I continued my search for a publisher, only to be rejected by at least ten more companies. Thankfully, after just six months of searching, I secured a publisher. The book was going to be more than an idea, a dream. It was going to be a reality. My reality.

The final piece of this serendipitous puzzle came almost one month to the day after signing my contract with Allworth Press, when I was given a chance to do my dream job. Now, I had been designing at universities, small regional theatres, large outdoor theatres, Fortune 500 companies, and high schools for over twenty years with well over one hundred designs on my résumé. Quite honestly, I'd already lived a life that I had only dreamed about as a child. Then, on August 8, 2011, I was asked to go to New York to serve as an assistant designer for the Broadway musical, *On a Clear Day You Can See Forever*. Because of a passing remark I'd made at the end of an interview—"If you ever need a Union design assistant, give me a call. I'd love to work with you"—I was on my way to Broadway.

I've shared this story with you for a couple of reasons. First, I had lived my life designing and teaching at a wonderful university with great colleagues. I was very happy working with students, helping them find their paths as young designers, and for *me* to get an opportunity to work on Broadway was beyond any dream I had ever had—even though when I was twenty-five years old I'd made a list of "goals" that I thought I should accomplish by the end of my career as a designer, and the last goal on my list was to work on Broadway (but this doesn't mean I'm calling it quits on my career). I had an idea that turned into a dream that turned into my reality.

My point is this: Dreams do not come true for those who are idle. Dreams do not come true for those who play it safe. Dreams do not come true for those who are unable to handle the pressure that comes with understanding that with great dreams comes great responsibility. I believe that dreams are not dreams at all—they are seeds of opportunity that you, or those who love you, have planted throughout your life. Sometimes those seeds grow into something unidentifiable, and we choose to pass them by. Other times, we pick them and discard them because we do not understand or appreciate their worth. And then there are those seeds that can blossom into the most beautiful flowers. Dreams are the seeds of opportunity. They are planted when you are hardworking, motivated, kind, talented, and, perhaps most of all, willing to step outside your comfort zone and experience life in a new and exciting way.

It is my hope that the stories contained in this book stand as examples that your dreams can take you wherever you want to go. This is the reality.

Michael Landman

"Courageously stating your goals and dreams aloud—ideally and with exquisite detail—makes them part of your future reality." —Michael Landman

Index